ESSENTIALS OF WOMEN RESOURCE DEVELOPMENT

Essentials of Women Resource Development

By
Trilok Singh

CYBER TECH PUBLICATIONS
4264/3, Ansari Road, Daryaganj, New Delhi-110002 (India)
Ph.: 011-23244078. Fax: 011-23280028
E-Mail: cyberpublicationsdelhi@yahoo.com

Essentials of Women Resource Development

Trilok Singh

First Edition 2011

Published by G.S. Rawat
For Cyber Tech Publications
4264/3, Ansari Road, Daryaganj, New Delhi-110002
Ph.: 011-23244078, 43559448 Fax: 011-23280028
E-Mail: cyberpublicationsdelhi@yahoo.com
E-mail: cybertechpublications@gmail.com
Website: www.cybertechpublications.com

Printed at
Asian offset printers.

Contents

Preface

> "In the humblest mortal there is throne room. Its door unfolds silently, magically, whenever one dares to be creatively useful; to benefit his kind by breaking new paths, building new structures, awakening new deeds and restoring new ideals."
>
> —*J.S. Von Goethe*

Human resource developed (HRD) is a necessary practice of modern management. Though 'human' in HRD stands for both male and female, in actual practice this is more man-centered. Hence the need of Women Resource Development (WRD), keeping in view the dilapidated condition of women resource.

Here in the present volume we have made an attempt to describe some salient features of the theme. The following chapters make core of our present venture—Introduction; Role of Education; Women As Human Resource; University Education Commission on Women; Women Resource Development: Institutional Efforts; Role of Women's Groups; Women Resource Development: Problems of Concepts and Assumptions; Developing Professionalism Among Women; Beijing Declaration (1995); Role of Liberation; The SAARC Decade Plan of Action for the Girl Child 1991-2000; Appendix & Bibliography.

Obviously this will delight and enlighten researchers, teachers, social scientists, policy planners and social and women activists besides NGOs and voluntary organizations operating in the field.

In course of furnishing authentic information, we have consulted a number of sources—both primary and secondary, and subscribed them by way of citation or substantial reproduction. I am deeply beholden to all the experts in the field whose views/works are made use of in this work. I am equally grateful to their publishers and copyright holders. Efforts are made to acknowledge them in references and bibliography.

Simultaneously I was much benefited by inspiration, guidance and assistance of my seniors, colleagues and friends. Besides these librarieans and other staff at different libraries has extended their cooperation by making available the requisite reading materials at their helms. I am thankful to them also.

Finally, I express my gratitude to my publishers for evincing keen interests in this project and also bringing out this on shortest possible time.

—Author

1

Introduction

> "Every man is to be respected as a absolute end in himself; and it is a crime against the dignity that belongs to him as a human being, to use him as a mere means for some external purpose."
>
> —*Immanuel Kant*

'Not gold but only men can make a nation great and strong' as H.W. Longfellow has said is now universally acclaimed. In fact men (human) resource is prime and prized asset of every nation.

About 54 per cent of India's population is in the working age-group of 15 to 59 years of age. In this age-group are there about 30 million officially registered unemployed persons. Even then we have not formulated any policy to utilise this huge amount of human resource directly. All our earlier policies has been indirectly aimed at employment generation as one of its aim. Even the Ministry of Human Resource Development still think in terms of providing education to the rural and urban population and how to improve the skills of the teachers.

This may solve the problem in future only and that too if a proper coordination takes place among various departments and the ministries. Why not the Ministry come out boldly on this issue? Let there be a policy which can say that those below secondary education should serve in the army compulsorily for a period of ten years and those completed secondary education for five years and so on. Needless, to mention about those who have not stepped into the schools and about the dropouts. Even in the advanced countries such as USA, and Germany this system exists, particularly for higher level posts in the government. When we can imitate all the other things from the West, why not this too? What prevents us from doing this?

However, for any kind of developmental activities one has to take of the availability of resources. The proper utilisation of resources are the most important aspects of planning. In this context, we have to take stock of the resources according to the types of resources.

Why Invest More in Women?

The Global HDR of UNDP 1995 noted, "Human development is a process of enlarging the choices for all people, not just one part of the society. Such a process becomes unjust and discriminatory if most women are excluded from its benefits. And the continuing exclusion of women from many economic and political opportunities is a continuing indictment of modern progress."

Experience has shown that the fruits of development, if invested in women, spread not only over a wider group of people, but also over a longer time span. Moreover, investing in women also entails a better and informed childcare, which can make a great difference in the growing up years of the child. Apart from these there remains the classic argument of multiplier effect that a gendered development perspective brings about in the overall development of a region.

The returns to society from investing in girls education are even larger and last for generations. Educated women have fewer children, and thus slow down the rate of population growth. They also tend to ensure better health and education for the future generations. The rate of return for girls' education is more than one percentage point higher than that for boys. The largest difference in returns comes from secondary education: 18.4 per cent for girls and 13.9 per cent for boys.

Women as Human Resource

In India, a high priority has been accorded to achieving economic development. Most of the developmental programmes and projects stress on an increase in national production. They squarely deal with fundamental issues of human equality, social justice, human resource development, etc. The development of the human potential by creating a better quality of human beings has not been substantially emphasised. Women development has remained all the more neglected. They have not been given the status of equality in the society. They are subjected to ill-treatment, socioeconomic injustice, exploitation and physical and mental torture.

Women constitute about 50 per cent of the population. Statistically speaking out of total literate population of 36.1 per cent, the percentage of literate males was nearly 47 per cent and the percentage of literate female was 25 per cent. This shows that the disparity in the literacy rate between males and females is very wide.

Figures of women's employment are very important indicators of the fact that the participation of women in the total work force of the country is actually decreasing. These statistical figures of women's employment are very important for the determination of women's status. The decline in the female participation in the total workforce over the past 60 years could be directly described to other factors which affect women adversly. One, there has been a fall in the female population compared with the male population. Two, there is an increasing gap between the male and female literacy rates in India. And three, the participation of the women in the decision-making body is declining.

Unfortunately, in spite of these depressing statistics it is also to be noted that though in terms of quantity the participation of women in the total labour force is declining in terms of quality, the diversity of occupations of which women can enter and are willing to enter irrespective of the traditionally or unconventiality of the occupations, is showing an upward trend. Several programmes have been formulated and implemented, but they have hardly changed employment status of women. What is more important is that a women needs freedom not from her own woman hood but from the centuries old shackles of injustice and discrimination.

For improving the status and to bring women into the mainstream women needs economic indepence. Not to be a burden on anyone can give a women immense self-confidence. Secondly, she needs to have an access to medical and health facilities. Fourthly, social evils like child marriage, child labour, purdah system, sati, and dowry which stand in the way of women's development should be removed. Fifthly, the attitude of women themselves has to be shaped to creative and positive thinking.

Suitable Strategies

In case of women development specially as human resource, some strategies are to be viewed holistically and not as isolated piecemeal actions. In order to be truly effective, the overall employment strategy for women should be viewed as a package comprising employment opportunities, legal safeguards, training support and social services, awareness generation and mobilisation. Only then will a purposeful synergy be achieved. The corrective strategies are broadly addressed to the factors which have been reviewed earlier as constraints.

Those strategies must aim to create new avenues for employment of women, upgrade their existing employment conditions as well as productivity and employment potential, make them a more articulate and conscious workforce, and assure them better status and recognition as workers.

Problem of Employment

As is generally being observed, the employment potential for women is likely to grow very slowly in the organised sector. On the other hand, there is a considerable scope for employment in the agricultural and service sectors. Diversification in agriculture and in the other major sectors of rural employment offers enormous potential for employment. Horticulture, commercial vegetable growing, food processing, fisheries and poultry, agro-industry offer ample opportunities to rural women.

Unemployed young women could be trained in extension work for importing the necessary skills in these activities. Besides, a variety of new occupations could be created for women workers in the areas of agro-based industry, weaving, textile printing, readymade garments, production of stationery and preparation of indigenous herbal medicines and packaging etc.

The service sector in the rural areas is a need and reality offering scope for local women to be absorbed with the minimum training being provided. Nurseries, creches and anganwadis also offer employment opportunities for a large number of women. The areas of simple health care like immunisation, diagnostic screening (testing of blood etc.) and other health functions could be opened to intermediary levels without affecting the overall standards. These facilities are not currently available to poor families particularly in the rural areas. Middle level workers could be trained for employment in the provision of these services.

There is an immediate need to diversify the prevailing occupational base so as to promote skilled employment on a wider scale. Currently, training is imparted in traditional occupations like carpentry, welding, smithing, tailoring, book binding etc. which is also male oriented. It is now necessary to provide training to women in such non-traditional fields as well.

An area based identification of potential occupational clusters would have to be undertaken systematically in different regions of the country in order to determine the nature and size of opportunities that could be made available. Effective linkages between metropolitan and large urban areas with the surrounding hinterlands is another modality with considerable potential for employment generation.

The demand from these urban and metropolitan centres in the fields of food processing, packaging, transportation, storage and other services could open up large areas for production, processing and marketing, thereby providing employment opportunities in such areas on a sizeable scale. Expansion of small-scale industries of widely recognised as a means of creating potential for employment.

Suitable institutional mechanism for the promotion of small scale industry need to be developed to assist in the provision of credit, supply of raw materials, organisation of marketing and creation of skills necessary for these enterprises. Two of the important areas requiring urgent attention for the expansion of cottage industries are— (i) Upgradation of skills in order to raise the status of workers to that of artisans and improve the quality of products; (ii) Education, training and organisations of workers for collective action on various issues. Appropriate technologies and modernisation of their occupations would have to be inducted to increase their income potential. The role of middlemen who have been getting sizeable benefits disproportionate to their investment and efforts has to be reduced. Producer Cooperatives are one such strategy to reduce dependence. An appraisal is necessary to examine the viability/ marketability of the trades for which training and assistance is being provided by the government.

The Central Social Welfare Board (CSWB) is implementing some employment generation schemes under which voluntary agencies in the country have been availing of financial assistance. Training is also given under TRYSEM etc. and socioeconomic schemes are undertaken under DWCRA, IRDP and the training-cum-production scheme of the Department of Women and Child Development, etc. An attempt should be made to expand the categories to encompass new and viable trades and create necessary linkages.

Training Issues

A systematic human resource development strategy focused on women is essential. Three levels of training are envisaged, viz. (i) The grass-roots level; (ii) The middle level; and (iii) The policy and planning level.

Componentsd of Training Strategy

- Organisational and extension training;
- Skill training;
- Management and entrepreneurial training;
- Sensitisation of administrators/implementors to women in development issues; and
- Training of trainers.

Components of training is to be geared to functionaries, catalysts, extension workers at the grass-roots, middle and supervisory level personnel, teachers, organisers of cooperatives, etc. It should aim at conscientisation on legislation, environmental health, nutrition and sanitation, education functional literacy, paralegal training and related aspects. Effective group mobilisation, communication skills, skills needed for organisation and management will be emphasised in this training alongwith functional knowledge. Particular attention should be paid to the attitudinal/ behavioural component essential for reaching programmes women at the grass-roots level.

Skill-Training

Refers to skill training with special emphasis on the nine major sectors of women's employment i.e. agriculture, dairying, fisheries, small animal husbandry, khadi and village industries, handicrafts, sericulture and social forestry. This type of training will entail upgrading existing skills in these areas as well as training of women in appropriate technologies. It will be aimed at programme beneficiaries as well as catalysts/functionaries, extension and supervisory workers. These skills need to be imparted on the widest scale to rural women in order to encourage them to achieve household self-sufficiency as well as supplementary income. Also included will be the skill training in the urban/modern sector with regard to assembly, manufacturing and processing for larger industries as well as small scale firms. Wherever possible women's employability has to be increased in the organised sector as the employment conditions in the unorganised sector indicate the need for a shift in the occupational structure.

In generating such skills, care will be taken to ensure that the training imparted does not push women into sectors where mobility is limited, wages are low, health hazards are high and worker benefits are not enforced.

Further, management training refers to training in project formulation, monitoring, evaluation, information systems, credit/marketing management, and other skills required to administer and manage projects, as well as supervisory and entrepreneurial skills. Such training could be provided with the help of technical institutes (ITIs, polytechnics, etc.) where special courses for training of women workers and entrepreneurs could be started. In conducting such courses, banks, voluntary organisations, and private and public sector industries could be effectively utilized to help formulate viable entrepreneurial projects for the trainees.

Special training programmes to promote rural entrepreneurship in particular would to be designed. Training should seek to achieve sensitisation of bureaucrats to the critical need to intergrate women in development. The objective will be to develop appropriate attitudes and knowledge for planning/monitoring/implementing programmes and policies for women.

Such training needs to be imparted through the training programmes of the Department of Personnel as well as other governmental and non-governmental agencies. A particular emphasis in this category of training must be to train the officers in charge of enforcement machineries at the Central and State levels, workers of quasi-governmental bodies, and voluntary agencies.

The Women's Division at NIPCCD is already undertaking sensitisation programmes for policy officers/ judiciary to the issues of crimes against women. In view of the criticality of training for the development of women, setting up of a National Resources Centre for Women is imperative. By playing a coordinating/interventionist role it would identify and strengthen existing governmental and non-governmental agencies to carry out training policy and programme research and information dissemination. The Resource-Centre would provide a new thrust for training and work towards translating national developmental goals into a systematic grid of programmes and schemes for training in skills/knowledge/attitudes at different levels. As a preparatory step, it would be essential to identify and classify the various types of training institutions in the country. Examples of such institutions are agriculture and rural home science centres; schools of social services, khadi and village industries, as well as vocational training centres; universities, ITIs, polytechnics, agriculture and veterinary schools, engineering college, krishi vigyan kendras, etc. At present, they have no special focus on training only for women, but these should take up new courses under a coordinated effort, monitored, and planned by the resource centre.

In addition, newly established training and extension departments, as well as existing training institutions, agencies, management bodies, and grass-roots organisations should be involved in imparting training to women. Once women are able to rise above the stereotyped roles assigned to them, they can contribute in achieving the goals of development, i.e. increasing the nation's GNP and per capita income, providing health for all by A.D. 2000, fulfilling the educational targets, etc. Which remained utopia till 2010. To achieve this, it is essential to provide a climate suitable for development of women. Isolated micro-level reforms would be a meaningless exercise in this context.

The Indian Constitution is firmly grounded in the principles of liberty, fraternity, equality and justice. It emphasises freedom for all and contains a number of provisions for the empowerment of women.

Women's right to equality and non-discrimination are guaranteed under the constitution. Further, it has been explicitly clarified that affirmative action programmes for women are not incompatible with the principle of non-discrimination on grounds of sex. India has reaffirmed its commitment to women by ratifying the UN conventions and international covenants like the CEDAW and Beijing Platform of Action. The Constitutional provisions and affirmations at the global level have unfortunately not translated into the intended status for women in the country.

Development in India and its states has not been equitable and men and women have benefited differently from development and progress, be it in the economic or on the political front. The social environment further exacerbates and reinforces this difference in development. The sex stereotypes in expected roles and responsibilities continue to perpetuate and reiterate this differential.

Although the development levels by the state are exemplary, the status of women continues to be a cause of concern. On the political, economic and social front, women have lagged behind not because they are not capable but because they have been denied opportunities even to survive.

The male-female sex ratio, the educational attainment levels, the infant mortality rates, the skilled workforce, access to common properties, right to inheritance are but a few indicators that highlight the differentials. At the same time, it is important to note that there has been a dramatic increase in the spaces available to women, many of which have been a consequence of state initiatives, through the formulation of gender-sensitive programmes, initiatives by NGOs and other civil society groups.

These changes have not come about in a single day.

Rather they have been the result of concerted efforts by women themselves. However, the critical issues that require to be addressed are increased violence against women and children in newer and more terrifying forms, the growing menace of identity-politics, the growing trend in economic policies which are eroding principles of distributive justice, growing environmental destruction, the continued marginalisation of women in public spheres and more importantly, from the areas of education, employment and better health services.

To draw attention to gender issues, UNDP's Global Human Development Report 1995 introduced the Gender Development Index (GDI) and Gender Empowerment Measure (GEM). GDI attempts to adjust the HDI for inequalities in the achievement of men and women. A comparison of a country's/state's ranking on the HDI and its ranking on the GDI can indicate the existence of gender discrepancy. GEM is a composite indicator that captures gender inequality in three key areas of political participation, economic participation and power over economic resources.

The GDI in itself is not a comprehensive tool to give a complete picture of gender equality and related concerns and issues but it does throw light on the situation of women. The various components, which have a direct bearing on gender equality and women's empowerment need to be studied in detail through demographic indicators, health, reproductive and child health, livelihoods, education. This chapter does that and brings out the inter and intra-state differentials.

Coming to the case of Punjab, as in other parts of India, Punjabi society consists of hierarchies based on caste, class and community. Within these hierarchies there is yet another hierarchy—of gender—women being at the lower rung. Generalisations on the condition of Punjabi women are almost impossible as there are sharp regional differences. There are many differences in health, literacy, education, sex ratio, rate of mortality, employment, incidence of poverty, political participation and so on.

The causes of such differences are, among others, pre-existing levels of development, availability or otherwise of natural resources, policies of the state government and regional norms and beliefs.

However, notwithstanding disparities, deprivation of women cuts across regions, classes and castes. For example, the success of the Green Revolution has pushed women, so far important contributors in the production process, back into the private domain. They lost their economic independence and their higher status within their class, because, with increased income and consequent higher social status for the families, women were the first to be withdrawn from the workforce as symbols of newly acquired status.

Certain development policies, or rather the lack of them, had severe consequences in creating newer disparities. There were marked differentials in labour force participation for poor women, both urban and rural. The state of rural women, who comprise the majority of the women's labour force, is pitiable. Most of them belong to the informal sector, with little or no bargaining power, which contributes to their marginalisation. This sector requires urgent action and intervention by the state.

Sikhism, Punjab's major religion, emphasises an egalitarian society. Sikh scriptures proclaim, "Why speak ill of those who give birth to kings?" But although in the realm of philosophy women are given equal, even elevated status, everyday realities tell a different story. Discrimination against girls and women seems to be woven into the very socio-cultural fabric of the society.

Furthermore, those 'God-fearing' persons who cannot practise female foeticide continue to have children till the woman bears a male child—her health not being a matter of concern. A woman's status in society, among her own peers is measured not by what she is and what she does but if she has at least one male child. So strong is this need to 'belong' to the society and community that women themselves perpetuate the custom of son preference.

In fact, the preference for the male child is strongly rooted in economics, particularly scarcity of agricultural resources, such as land. Since women have been largely left out of the agricultural process, land and its use have become a typically male domain. Any woman trying to get her share of the ancestral property was accused of being vile, base and depraved. A number of customs can be traced to efforts at keeping valued assets within the family. Widows were married off to younger brothers-in-law through a practice known as '*chadar pauna*'. Sisters were discouraged from asking for their share in property and any actions in this direction invariably led to rift in family ties. Women were thus discouraged from claiming any rights to land or assets of value. The post-1975 period saw awareness among women about rights, particularly inheritance rights. Now women are making headway forward. They are not only home-maker but occupying top positions in corporate sector. Many successful women are there listed as famous top corporate leaders.

But this large pool of womenpower as human resource is not yet fully exploited. Women in rural areas are still far behind. Concerted efforts are to be made to turn womenpower in useful human resource. A long course is yet to the traversed in this direction.

Here in this book we will address all such issues which are the major components of women as human resource.

In next chapter we will elicidate the role of education and training.

REFERENCES

Govt. of India (1988): *National Perspective Plan for Women* 1983 - 2000 A.D., Min. of HRD, Deptt. of Women & Child Development, New Delhi, p. 5.

Sapru Sushma, (1989): 'Socio-economic Status of Women: Problems and Perspectives,' in R.K. Sapru (Ed.), *Women and Development,* Ashish Publishing House, New Delhi, p. 235.

Shridharan N., (1989): Whither Democratic Planning: Some Issues,' in Ashok Kumar and R.P. Mamgain (ed.), *Manpower Planning in India,* Criterion Publications, New Delhi, p. 29.

2

Role of Education

> "Education is not intended to make lawyers or clergymen, soldiers or schoolmasters, farmers or artisans but men."
>
> —*Sir John Lubbock*

Skill and proficiency in any profession can be developed by proper education and training. These are the prerequisites of human resource development. Women lagged far behind in this matter hence they could not be turned into useful human resource despite huge probability and potential.

Education is the most important instrument for human resource development. Education of women, therefore, occupies top priority amongst various measures taken to improve the status of women in India. In recent years, the focus of planning has shifted from equipping women for their traditional roles of house-wives and mothers to recognising their worth as producers, making a major contribution to family and national income.

Efforts have been made over the past three decades of planned development to enrol more girls in schools and encourage them to stay in schools, to continue their education as long as possible, and to provide non-formal educational opportunities for women.

The fulfilment of the Constitutional directives in respect of providing free and compulsory education upto the age of 14 years has been included as one of the components of the 'Minimum Needs Programme' and given over-riding priority. Education in India is constrained by the socioeconomic conditions of the people their attitudes, values and culture. During the pre-British era, education was linked to the socio-religious institutions, reinforcing the patriarchal social structure. During the British period, education became a tool of colonial power, enabling a small minority to have access to education, and all the benefits it entailed. The social reformers of the 19th century raised the demand for women's transformation but to make them more capable of fulfilling their traditional roles. Since independence, the policy makers have argued for universal education and for making education as a tool for bringing about social equality. In spite of concerted efforts to improve the enrolment of girls and provide adult education for women, their educational status is still far from satisfactory. Female enrolment in educational institutions is low as when compared with males and dropout rates are high. There are also regional and inter-group disparities. The factors which do not permit the closing of the existing gap between the education of men and women are many.

While undertaking a review of the educational system at the time of formulation of the National Policy on Education 1986, it was noted that the system is caught in a state of ambivalence, aiming at creating an equal society while at the same time not disturbing the class, caste and gender relationships. Issues in women's education are, therefore, not issues only of educational sector, but they extend to issues of environment, employment, production processes. Indeed, the entire gamut of social and economic policy has a bearing on women's education. The need for educating girls is not considered worthwhile. In urban areas, by and large, there is a greater acceptance of its need than in rural areas.

Causes of Low Enrolment

- The requirement for older girls to stay at home to take care of siblings when mothers are away at work;
- Need for girls to work in order to help in a augmenting the family income;
- Early marriage of girls;
- Social customs that hinder female mobility after puberty;
- Lack of relevance of school curriculum, and
- Lack of facilities in the form of school buildings, hostels and women teachers etc.

Strategy Adopted

Women's education has assumed special significance in the context of the country's planned development. This is because women constitute nearly half the nation's population representing a valuable human resource, and play an important role in the development of the community and the national economy. Education enables women to acquire basic skills and abilities, and fosters a value system which is conducive to raising their status in society. Recognising this fact, great emphasis has been laid on women's education in the Five-Year Plans.

The First Five-Year Plan advocated the need for adopting special measures for solving the problems of women's education. It held that women "must have the same opportunities as men for taking all kinds of work and this presupposes that they get equal facilities so that their entry into the professions and public services is in no way prejudiced".

It further added that "at the secondary and even at the university stage it should have a vocational or occupational basis, as far as possible, so that those who complete such stages may be in a position, if necessary, to immediately take up some vocation or other". Accordingly, the educational facilities for girls continued to expand in the subsequent plans. The major schemes undertaken encompassed elementary education, secondary education, university education, post-graduate education and research, technical education, scholarships, social/adult education and physical education. The Second Plan continued the emphasis on overall expansion of educational facilities.

The Report of the National Committee on Women's Education (1959) made a strong impact on the Third Five-Year Plan. It launched important schemes like condensed school courses for adult women. Bal Sevika training and child care programmes. Subsequent plans supported these measures and also continued incentives such as free textbooks and scholarships for girls. This trend continued in the Fourth and Fifth Five-Year Plans. Although there was a large scale expansion of facilities for education upto the Fourth Plan vast disparities existed in the relative utilisation of available facilities by boys and girls at various stages of education. Hence, the major thrust in the Fifth Plan was to offer equality of opportunities as part of the overall plan of ensuring social justice and improving the quality of education imparted. To promote enrolment and retention in schools in backward areas and among under-privileged sections of the population, in addition to the incentives like free distribution of text-books, mid-day meals etc., girls were to be given uniforms and attendance scholarships.

In spite of these schemes, it was noticed that insufficient numbers of women teachers resulted in low enrolment of girls. To remove this bottleneck, scholarships were given to local girls to complete their education and training leading to a teaching career. Besides, condensed and correspondence courses were organised for the less educated women. Emphasis was also laid on the need for orientation of the curriculum to meet the special needs of girls.

Significantly, a landmark in the Sixth Plan was the inclusion of women's education as one of the major programmes under Women and Development which was an outcome of the publication of the report of the Committee on the Status of Women in India. The programmes for universalisation of elementary education were specially directed towards higher enrolment and retention of girls in schools. It was envisaged to promote balwadi-cum-creches attached to the schools to enable girls responsible for sibling care at home to attend schools.

Women teachers, where necessary, were to be appointed in rural areas to encourage girls' education. Science teaching in girls schools and colleges had to be strengthened to achieve greater participation of women in science and technology. Streamlining the admission policies to promote greater enrolment of women in engineering, electronics, agriculture, veterinary, fishery and forestry courses was stressed.

For boosting the education of women belonging to backward classes, the number of girl's hostels were to be increased. Instead of adding more separate women's polytechnics, which were developed as multi-purpose institutions for imparting training in arts, crafts, etc., co-educational institutions were encouraged as far as possible. The adult education programme too received a fillip. The Seventh Plan envisages restructuring of the educational programmes and modification of school curricula to eliminate gender bias. Enrolment of girls in elementary, secondary and higher education courses, formal as well as non-formal, has been accorded high priority. At the elementary stage, education has been made free for girls. Sustained efforts are to be made through various schemes and measures to reach 100 per cent coverage in elementary education. Financial assistance schemes to voluntary agencies to run early childhood education (pre-school centres) as adjuncts of primary/middle schools are to be expanded, particularly to help evolve innovative models suited to specific learner groups or areas.

Efforts are to be made to enrol and retain girls in schools, especially in rural areas, and also to enrol children belonging to scheduled castes, scheduled tribes and other weaker sections. Teacher training programmes are to receive continued priority with a view to increase the availability of trained women teachers, and thereby to enhance girl's enrolment and retention in schools.

Incentives by way of distribution of uniforms, free text books and attendance scholarships to needy girls are to be continued. Non-formal elementary education is to be expanded to benefit girls in the age-group of 6-14 years. Talented girls are to be encouraged to pursue higher education. It is also proposed to expand the 'Open Learning System', including correspondence courses for them. In order to promote technical and vocational education for girls, more women's polytechnics are to be set up and programmes for vocationalisation of education are to be expanded. To expedite education among the girls of the scheduled castes and scheduled tribes, additional facilities will continue to be provided under the "Development of Backward Classes" sector. Girls above the matriculation stage will get higher scholarships/stipends than boy students.

Financial assistance is envisaged for construction of hostel buildings for girls at the district level and for purchase of equipment, furniture utensils, books and periodicals in these hostels. Under the National Sports Policy, participation of women and girls in sports and games is to be encouraged. Stress is to be laid on the identification of sports talent among women, and provision made for sports scholarships, coaching and nourishment support for promising girls with a view to improve the standards of their performance in competitive games.

Apart from the schemes for encouraging traditional folk, tribal and hill arts and cultural activities are to be expanded and strengthened.

An Evaluation

Notwithstanding the planned objectives and endeavours, actual progress in upgrading the educational status of women has been slow. The literacy level among women has risen from 7.9 per cent in 1951 to 24.3 per cent in 1981 (excluding Assam). Among males, the corresponding rise was from 24.9 to 46.3 per cent. Thus the gap in percentage literacy points between male and female literacy increased from 17 in 1951 to 22 in 1981. In absolute terms too, the number of illiterate women has increased during the period, from 158.7 million to 241.7 million (excluding Assam). Women comprised 57 per cent of the illiterate population in 1981, and girls formed 70 per cent of non-enrolled children in the school age group. There are disturbing regional variations in the levels of literacy in the country. The literacy rate for women varies from 65.7 per cent in Kerala, as per 1981 census, to 11.4 per cent for Rajasthan. The Gap between male and female literacy rates in percentage points in only 9.5 in Kerala, but 24.9 in Rajasthan. States like Madhya Pradesh, Uttar Pradesh and Bihar are also lagging behind in girl's education. Certain ecological constraints like difficult terrain, variety of dialects as in Arunachal Pradesh, migratory habits due to inclement weather as in parts of Jammu and Kashmir etc., have also been instrumental in perpetuating low levels of literacy in such areas for the population as a whole and particularly for women.

Now we will assess the problem at different le3vels of education. First the elementary education.

1. Elementary Education

In fact, high priority has been accorded to elementary education in the National Development Plans to fulfil the requirements under Article 45 of the Constitution for universal free and compulsory elementary education for children upto the age of 14 years. Progressive rise in the enrolment ratio i.e. the percentage of children enrolled to their total population in the age group during the various Plan periods is apparent.

By the end of the Sixth Plan, it was apparent that in order to achieve universal elementary education, an additional enrolment of 255.3 lakhs is required of which the girls constitute 140.7 lakhs i.e. a little more than 55 per cent. Besides, there is a sharp fall in the number of girls enrolled at primary level to the number enrolled at the middle level viz., from nearly 32 lakhs of 91 lakhs indicating a large dropout rate, wastage and stagnation. The enrolment ratio falls from 76.7 to 36.3. The retention of girls in schools from I to VIII class, therefore is a task requiring urgent attention. Among Scheduled Tribes (ST) particularly, the enrolment of girls is far below that of boys. At the primary stage, the enrolment of ST boys is almost double the enrolment of girls, and the difference increases at higher stage. Girls belonging to Scheduled Castes (SC) communities are also lagging behind boys. The ratio of SC boys to girls in the elementary classes is 2:1. In the VI to VIII classes, 61.9 per cent of girls in the general population are enrolled, whereas among the SCs this proportion is only 29.9 per cent. The reasons for SC and ST girls lagging behind the boys are mainly rooted in socio-economic conditions and environmental constraints such as inaccessibility of schools in tribal areas. Irrelevance of formal education curriculum to the immediate environment is also responsible for low initial enrolment and subsequent dropout rates. Among the urban and rural poor, the compulsion on girls to assist in household chores including care of younger siblings, and on children of both sexes to work for their own survival and contribute economically to the household income, forces them to remain outside the education system.

According to the Fourth Educational Survey (1978), in the plains 95 per cent of the rural population have access to a primary school within one kilometer of their habitation (having a population of 300 persons or more). Middle schools are available to 78.8 per cent of rural people within three kilometers from their habitation. But commuting to distant schools does pose a problem for girls. There are very few separate schools for girls. The parents, particularly in rural areas, are reluctant to send their daughter to co-educational schools. Moreover, in most schools, the teachers are male. Despite considerable emphasis in the plans, the proportion of women teachers continues to be low. Provision for accommodation for women workers including teachers is far from satisfactory. A large number of primary and middle schools, in rural areas especially, lack facilities such as a proper building, adequate number of teaching rooms, drinking water and toilets for girls. More than 85 per cent primary and 70 per cent middle schools in rural areas do not have this facility, according to the Fourth All India Educational Survey (1978). Hostel facilities for girls continue to be meagre.

2. Secondary Education

Remarkably, the enrolment ratio of girls in the age group 15-18 years for secondary classes is 14.3 per cent as against 29.3 per cent for boys. Secondary education continues to be more or less confined to urban areas, and is affordable and accessible largely to the higher castes and the upper and middle economic strata. Although a large number of secondary schools have come up in rural areas, their enrolment, particularly, in respect of girls is low. The main constraints in improving secondary and higher level education among girls have been a lack of availability of trained lady teachers, dearth of separate institutions for girls and lack of hostel facilities. The 10+2+3 system of education has been introduced with the aim of establishing a uniform pattern of education all over the country in terms of its structure, curriculum and mobility across the States.

This system has laid a common foundation for higher education without differentiation between boys and girls. Both girls and boys under the new system will learn the rudiments of science and mathematics, social sciences and humanities upto matriculation and thus gain a holistic basic education which will equip them to play an active and meaningful role in the employment market of today.

3. Higher Education

It is pertinent to note that the higher educational courses, girls constitute 24 to 50 per cent of the students enrolled, depending upon the type of courses. The most popular course with girls has been teachers training where they already constitute nearly fifty per cent of those enrolled. The number of girls in science courses had risen to 41 per 100 boys in 1984-85. In engineering and technology courses, however, the enrolment of girls is only 6 for 100 boys.

This proportion has to be enhanced through suitable incentives in the forms of scholarships and other facilities for girls studying for these courses. Girls enrolled for higher education, particularly those in science and technical courses, are mainly from the higher economic strata. There is a need to introduce positive measures to improve the enrolment to girls in higher education courses in rural areas and among backward groups like SCs and STs and other backward classes.

4. Non-formal Education

Basically, the concept of adult education has found support in several plan programmes. However, until the Sixth Plan, no special emphasis was given to women's education. In the Sixth Five-Year Plan, adult education was included as a part of the "Minimum Needs Programme' and the goal of reaching 100 per cent literacy by 1990 was set under the New Twenty Point Programme. Adult education centres exclusively for women were set up, which provided education in subjects like health, nutrition and family planning.

An effort was made to build up awareness about these subjects among women through discussions, talks, and distribution of relevant literature. Under the Adult Education Programme, apart from increasing adult literacy, the content of education was to be modified to incorporate new value systems regarding the role of women in the family and community. The Seventh Plan also envisages, among other schemes, the preparation of district level plans with local community participation both for activating and implementing the literacy programme, and the creation of special mechanisms to monitor the progress of implementation at the State level.

The Integrated Rural Development Programme (IRDP), National Rural Employment Programme (NREP), Training of Rural Youth in Self-Employment (TRYSEM), and other such programmes, are also to have a component of functional literacy for women beneficiaries. The programme of Functional Literacy for Adult Women (a component of the ICDS programme) was unfortunately abandoned, though the concept of utilising Anganwadi workers, who belonged to the villages and were in contact with young mothers, could have been an effective mechanism for imparting non-formal education. The scheme has since been revised to focus on issues of immediate relevance to women but has yet to be introduced. The scheme of 'condensed courses of education and vocational training' for adult women was started in 1958 under the aegis of the Central Social Welfare Board, and was suitably expanded over the years to vocational training in areas with high employment potential.

Measures are to be taken to enhance the competence of the teaching staff/training institutions involved in this programme. The various programmes, however have not yet been able to make any significant impact on literacy levels of the Indian population, particularly on women. According to a World Bank Report, in 2000 A.D. there were 500 million illiterates in India, constituting 54 per cent of the world's population of illiterates. As per the Seventh Plan, the total number of adult illiterates is about 900 lakhs, of whom 580 lakhs are women. Although it is encouraging to note that the proportion of women in the adult education centres has gone above 50 per cent (52.34

per cent in 1984-85), women still constitute about 57 per cent of the illiterate population. Among these, literacy levels of SC and ST women are still worse. Even those treated as literates, have very low levels of literacy scant opportunities of continuing education and use of literacy skills. Therefore, they often relapse into illiteracy.

National Policy on Education—Initiatives for Women

It is significant to note that the National Policy on Education (NPE)-1986 is a landmark in the approach to women's education. It has attempted for the first time to address itself to the basic issues of women's equality. In the section titled "Education for Women's Equality," the policy states:

> "Education will be used as an agent of basic change in the status of women. In order to neutralise the accumulated distortions of the past, there will be a well-conceived edge in favour of women. The National Education System will play a positive, interventionist role in the empowerment of women. It will foster the development of new values through redesigned curricula, textbooks, training and orientation of teachers, decision-makers and administrators."

It gives over-riding priority to the removal of women's illiteracy and obstacles inhibiting their access to and retention in elementary education. Emphasis has been laid on women's participation in vocational, technical and professional education at different levels as also to promote women's participation in non-traditional occupations and existing and emergent technologies.

"Women become empowered through collective reflection and decision-making. The parameters of empowerment are:

- Building a positive self-image an self-confidence;
- Developing ability to think critically;

- Building up group cohesion and fostering decision-making and action;
- Ensuring equal participation in the process of bringing about social change;
- Encouraging group action in order to bring about change in the society;
- Providing the wherewithal for economic independence..."

The programme entails the following:

(i) A phased time bound programme of elementary education for girls, particularly upto primary stage by 1990 and upto the elementary stage by 1995.

(ii) A phased time bound programme of adult education for women in the age-group 15-35 by 1995.

(iii) Increased women's access to vocational, technical, professional education and existing and emergent technologies and

(iv) Review and re-organisation of educational activities to ensure that they make a substantial contribution towards women's equality, and creation of appropriate cells/units therefor.

As such, a number of measures have been suggested to achieve the stated objectives of the National Policy on Education. The Action Plan enunciates that every educational institution should take up by 1995 active programmes for the development of women. All teachers and non-formal education/adult education instructors should be trained as agents of women's development. Special programmes should be developed by research institutions to promote general awareness and positive self-image amongst women through programmes like discussions, street plays, wall papers, puppet shows, etc. Preference in recruitment of teachers upto school level should be for women. National Literacy Mission (NLM) which aims at eradication of illiteracy in 15-35 age-group by 1995 concretises what is envisaged in NPE as regards literacy and adult education. The Mission document emphasises the importance of imbibing the values of national integration, conservation of environment, women's equality, observance of small family norm etc. and goes on to say that "the focus of NLM would be on rural areas, particularly women and persons belonging to the Scheduled Castes and Scheduled Tribes." For universalisation of elementary and adult education, the present programme of non-formal centres for girls needs to be extended to all educationally backward pockets of the country.

Increased assistance should be given to voluntary organisations to run non-formal education centres for girls. In rural areas, special support services should be provided to relieve the girls from sibling care and other household work like fetching water, fuel, etc. Skill development linked to employment opportunities in the villages is required to be given priority so that there is an incentive on the part of the parents to educate girls. It is necessary to develop adult education programmes for women linked with ugradation of their skills and income generating activities.

Skill development for girls should be a continuous process of learning and should be supported by programmes administered by other agencies such as poly-technics, Industrial Training Institutes (ITIs), Women's Centres in Agricultural and Home Science Colleges, etc. Continuing Education Centres should be set up in a phased manner to organise vocational training, provide opportunities for retention of literacy skills, and application of this learning for improving their living conditions. There were 104 ITIs functioning exclusively for women and 97 wings in general ITIs reserved for women. These would need to be revamped during 1988-90 in terms of diversification of trades and courses, keeping in view the job potential, and facilities for vocational counselling, imparting information about credit, banking, entrepreneurial development and women's access to technical education, etc.

Further, women's studies programmes would also have four dimensions, viz. teaching, research, training and extension. Women's issues would be incorporated in courses under various disciplines. Research would be encouraged on identified areas/subjects. Seminars/workshops would be orgnised on the need for women's studies, and for dissemination of information and interaction.

Educational institutions would be encouraged to take up programmes like adult education, awareness building, legal literacy, information and training support for socio-economic programmes of women's development, instructional programmes through media, etc., which directly benefit the community and bring about the empowerment of women. All the forgoing endeavours will be planned, coordinated, monitored and evaluated continuously both at the national and state levels. The Women's Cell in the National Council for Educational Research and Training would be revived and strengthened. National Institute of Educational Planning and Administration and Directorate of Adult Education would have cells to plan and administer women's training programmes.

The Women's Cell in the University Grants Commission would be strengthened to monitor the implementation of various programmes at the higher education level. It is proposed that women's cells should be set up in all the states.

The programmes for women's education will have to be

implemented as a priority so that women attain a comparable level of education by 2000 A.D. The strategy to be adopted for raising literacy levels and education among women has to keep in view the vast cultural, geographical and ecological variations as also the problems relating to poverty and ignorance. The cultural and geographical variations call for decentralisation of educational planning. Within the national perspective, planning, implementation and monitoring of educational programmes has to be done at district and block levels, keeping in view the socio-economic and geographic parameters of the area. The vocational and occupational components have to be designed in accordance with the availability of resources and job opportunities in the regions.

Voluntary organisations and women's groups active in the area should be involved in the task. In view of the social and cultural handicaps that have operated against women's education and taking account of the multiple roles that women are required to play, the need for adopting a set of objectives specific to women's education is imperative

Main Objectives

- Elimination of illiteracy, universalisation of elementary education and minimisation of the dropout rate in the age-group 6-14 years and stagnation to negligible proportions.
- Ensuring opportunities to all women for access to appropriate level, nature and quality of education and also the wherewithal for success comparable with men.
- Substantial vocationalisation and diversification of secondary education so as to provide a wide scope for employment and economic independence of women.

- Making education an effective means for women's equality by (a) Addressing ourselves to the constraints that prevent women from participating in the educational process; (b) Eliminating the existing sexist bias in the system; (c) Making necessary intervention in the content and processes of education to inculcate positive and egalitarian attitudes, and (d) Ensuring that teacher's perceive this as one of their essential roles.
- Providing non-formal and part-time courses to women to enable them to acquire knowledge and skills for their social, cultural and economic advancement.
- Impetus to enrol in various professional degree courses so as to increase their number in medicine, teaching, engineering and other fields substantially.
- Creating a new system of accountability, particularly in respect of the basic educational services, to the local community, inter alia, by active involvement of women.

Briefly, it is reiterated that the goals and strategies spelt out in the National Policy on Education, POA and the National Literacy Mission will ensure a much larger access for women to education. High priority has to be accorded to creating awareness, through the various communication media, of the need for women's' education and their active participation in economic and political development of the nation. The curricula for school as well as university education have to be reviewed and revised so as to remove sex bias, inculcate among the masses a recognition of equality between men and women, and make women aware of their own potential as well as provide them necessary opportunities to develop their capabilities in every field.

Greater accessibility of educational facilities to girls is to be achieved by reducing the distance of schools from village habitations, and expanding non-formal elementary education, adult education, and the open school system. Appointment of lady teachers in schools would help draw more girls to schools and instil confidence among their parents. Towards this end, provision of quarters for lady teachers would be essential. Efforts should be directed at training local women as teachers.

Provision of creche facilities and balwadis near the elementary and secondary schools for girls would enable the girls to attend schools and ensure care of younger siblings. Incentives like mid-day meals; better rates of scholarships, freeships, etc. would go a long way in preventing dropout. Above all, better health facilities, smaller families, and relief from drudgery through improved technology for household chores, are essential pre-requisites for better enrolment of girls at schools and higher educational institutions.

Inputs from other sectors are, therefore, important. Greater coordination of health, employment, welfare and education interventions will have an effect on the status of women and girls. According to Educational Statistics for 1984-85 published by the Ministry of Human Resource Development, the enrolment of girls at primary level, which covers the age group 6-11 years, is 331.9 lakhs. Surveys and field research have pointed out that there is 25 per cent inflation in the enrolment figures, and 22 per cent enrolment is outside the age groups. Thus the effective enrolment gets reduced by about 47 per cent. Accordingly, the coverage for 1984-85 for the 6-11 years age group may be estimated as 176 lakhs. The population projected for the age-group is 422.7 lakhs. This means that only 40.7 per cent of the girls in the age group 6-11 are enrolled in schools. On a similar basis, the enrolment of 11-14 years age group gets reduced to 48.1 lakhs (from 90.7 lakhs) which is only 19.2 per cent of the population of 249.9 lakhs estimated for the age group. The population projections for the girls in the age group 6-11 years and 11-14 years for 1989-90 are 462 lakhs and 267 lakhs respectively.

In order to have full coverage, the additional enrolment required would be 286 lakhs for 6-11 age group and 219 lakhs for 11-14 years age group, the total being nearly 5 crores. The task appears to be stupendous. Alongwith enrolment, there is the problem of very high dropout rates. Stemming from highly inflated enrolment rates and subsequent dropouts in the 6-11 years age group, enrolment of 11-14 years age group girls, even at primary level, may not be possible even by 1995.

Remarkably, in view of the social and cultural handicaps that have operated against women's education, the need for a adopting a set of objectives specific to women's education is imperative. These would need to encompass the elimination of illiteracy and measures for retention of girls in schools, substantial vocationalisation and diversification to enhance economic opportunities for women, improvement in the quality of education in terms of the values it promoters and inculcates, and finally the provision of access to professional courses for women.

Such measures would be necessary as also efforts to remove the inherent prejudices working against women's education. Awareness needs to be generated among the masses regarding the necessity of educating girls so as to prepare them to effectively contribute to the socio-economic development of the country, to strengthen their role in society and to realise their own capacities.

The media and various forms of communication have to be geared to this end. A fruitful rapport has to be established between the community at large and the teachers and other education personnel. As per the Programmes of Action under National Policy on Education-1986, every educational institution should actively participate in bringing about such awareness. Involvement of local leaders, voluntary agencies and women's groups is also necessary.

Mahila mandals need to be *revitalised* and re-oriented to provide an effective forum for the purpose. One measure to achieve this could be to assign the responsibility to mahila mandals for ensuring that all children in a community attend school. An incentive scheme should be introduced to motivate panchayats to ensure 100 per cent enrolment of girls in their respective villages. Early childhood care and education introduces children into the school system gradually and smoothly. When children get used to attending schools, it ensures in some measures retention of children, including girls, at elementary stages also.

Hence there is need to have a comprehensive and effective programme of early childhood care and education linked to an integrated package of learning of women. The most comprehensive example of this is the Integrated Child Development Services Programme which needs to be universalised. For improving enrolment and minimising drop-outs and wastage in case of girl students, it would be helpful if learning is made more attractive by providing adequate teaching materials in schools. The number of teachers should also be increased so that the interaction between the teacher and the taught, which is so essential for good education, also increases.

This would help in the retention of girls in schools and would be more effective if teachers from the area are employed. In single teachers schools, the teacher must be a woman. In the case of two-teacher schools, at lest one teacher must be a woman. In Orissa all jobs of primary teachers have been reserved for women. School curricula should be imaginatively developed to stimulate creativity largely through play rather than overburdening children with formal or rote learning. Regional language should normally be the medium of instruction. School timings should be flexible and fixed to suit local conditions and the needs of the working girl and must be available within the walking distance of the child.

A substantial increase is required in the number of schools for girls. In addition to incentives like free textbooks, free supply of uniforms, award of attendance scholarships and mid-day meals, facilities such as proper school building, safe drinking water, and toilets, etc. need to be provided to encourage school enrolment and retention of girls especially girls from educationally deprived social groups and from hilly, tribal, desert and remote rural areas and urban slums. Local talent must be developed in order to meet the need for recruiting women teachers at the primary and elementary levels especially in rural and tribal areas. In this endeavour national agencies like CAPART and CSWB, voluntary agencies, mahila mandals and local self-government agencies can make a significant contribution. They can also play a useful watchdog function to ensure that educational and other programmes are run efficiently and effectively. There should be a reservation of 50 per cent posts for women teachers in elementary schools. Women teachers working in the rural areas should be provided suitable accommodation. Multi-entry system for girls who cannot attend schools continuously should be adopted. Wherever necessary, schools meant exclusively for girls may be set up. The recommended distance of 3 kilometers for locating a middle school is a handicap for many girls. To ensure participation of girls in middle schools, it is necessary to provide hostel facilities.

Remarkably, the Savitribai Phule Foster Parent Scheme of Maharashtra could be adopted in other States/Union Territories to help girls of poorer families to at least compete primary school. Under the scheme, well to do persons and organisations are persuaded to adopt one or more out of school girls and contribute in cash or kind or both @Rs. 25 per month for her education. The money can be spent on uniforms, stationary or anything else, needed by the girl or also partly used to alleviate the economic distress of the parents. The Zila Parishad, Block Education Officer and headmasters play a pivotal role in implementing the scheme, which is purely voluntary and if district level officers for coordination of programmes for women are appointed they could also actively take it up.

Condensed courses of education at elementary and middle school levels for girls must be started in all the rural areas and for weaker sections of the urban community. Many girls in the 11-14 years age group would first have to be brought into the primary stage through non-formal education. By devising alternative education approaches non-formal schooling and through like intelligent use of technology, the pace of middle school education can be accelerated. If retention upto 75 per cent is achieved upto class V, universal elementary education may be possible in some parts of the country by 2000 A.D.

Other backward areas would have to be given much more attention in professional as well as financial terms to enable them even to universalise primary education for girls by 1995. The National Literacy Mission will need to address these issues on a priority basis. Special efforts are necessary for bringing tribal children particularly, girls into the school system. Tribal dialects, extreme poverty, problems of commuting, rigidity of formal education and its irrelevance to the tribal culture and the tribals' distrust of the ways of the mainstream society, must be borne in mind in formulating strategies. The educational forecasts, may look more achievable if the system is opened up for flexible non-formal education which 'the below average states' should be persuaded to adopt in a large measure.

The existing educational infrastructure particularly, in tribal and rural areas should be made effective and responsible. Non-formal education is an alternative to the formal system which has the potentiality of becoming the major programme of education for girls who cannot attend school during normal school hours due to various reasons. The Central Government is already implementing a centrally-sponsored scheme under which grants to the extent of 90 per cent are provided towards maintenance of non-formal education centres exclusively for girls in nine educationally backward states.

This programme should be strengthened further and extended to other states where education of girls is lagging behind. It should at least cover all the pockets of low enrolment of girls and areas of high dropout rate. Besides literacy, it must also provide relevant information on skill development and inculcation of positive self-image among girls.

Secondary education for girls should entail:

> (i) A ten year course in general education learning and diversified higher secondary education which may be either terminal or lead to further professional preparation; and
> (ii) Diversified courses after Grade VIII in technical subjects viz., agricultural technology, health services, food production

activities such as, dairy and poultry and non-traditional areas need to be untroubled. A legal literacy component is also recommended at this stage.

Diversified courses leading to occupational preparation should be of parallel duration to the general secondary courses. In addition, there should be a variety of short and long-term, whole time, part-time and apprentice courses. The trend of thinking is now to place emphasis on the last. Keeping in view the rapid modernisation and advancement in technology for agriculture, there is an urgent need for skilled artisanship for promoting productive activities on the one hand, and a variety of learning programmes for adjustment of the rural society to social-economic change, on the other.

Efforts should be made to ensure that girls have every opportunity to enter into apprenticeship in areas that are non-conventional, and incentives be provided for the same. Further, at least 30 per cent seats should be reserved for girls in apprenticeship training courses on a non-transferable basis. General and vocational training courses should be combined so that prospects of a career immediately on completion of schooling may attract girls from weaker sections.

While designing the vocational courses, available occupational opportunities as well as the need to overcome market stereotypes should be kept in view. Since secondary education has remained almost beyond the reach of weaker sections, liberal incentives and other facilities to release the girls from household chores appear to be essential. It would also help to locate the institutions in the areas of their habitation. Multiple entry system should be introduced in the secondary facilities should also be made available.

Condensed courses should be organised in cooperation

with local vocational training institutions to cover all rural areas and areas inhabited by weaker sections in urban areas. Such courses may be organised for small groups of girls, and combined with job training. Efforts should be made to cover at least 215 lakhs women in the age-group 15-30 years under the condensed courses programme wherever possible the condensed courses of the CSWB should be expanded and strengthened. New programmes that are to be initiated must avoid duplication in the area where the CSWB's programmes exists. Correspondence courses and self study programme can be especially useful for girls desirous of continuing education but are unable to do so because of circumstances.

Apart from imparting elementary education and knowledge about farming techniques, the curriculum for non-student girls should include courses of training in occupational skills. Similar programmes should also be designed for girls in the urban areas. The open school system should be expanded extending the facility to all the girls in rural and backward areas. Science education for girls has been neglected so far. Secondary schools for girls must be helped to build good science programmes over the Eighth Five-Year Plan. Special scholarships for girls opting for science courses need to be instituted at the secondary and higher education levels.

Special scholarships may also be offered to rural women, who opt for teachers training, especially those who complete the condensed courses at the secondary stage. There is a need to open more colleges and polytechnics for girls, especially in rural areas.

Incentives like scholarships, freeships, etc., should be provided to enable girls from rural areas to pursue higher education for girls belonging to weaker sections. In addition to freeships and scholarships bursaries should also be provided to meet their requirements for food and lodging. Girls should be encouraged to enter professional courses. Reservation of seats for girls in such courses may be considered to level out the existing bias in access to certain professional streams.

Vocational counselling and guidance service should be organised exclusively in a more meaningful way to help girls in colleges and universities opt for suitable courses relevant to their talents and interests, and free of traditional bias.

In fact, vocational and technical education for women, both formal and nonformal, should be a major feature of the programmes of rural universities. The women's wings of the universities could undertake larger scale extension programmes in order to activate girls and women in the surrounding areas to take advantage of educational and occupational facilities of various types, particularly those leading to meaningful employment, essential for reducing women's marginalilsation'. In order to increase the representation of rural girls in higher education courses, 30 percent seats, may be reserved for girls to begin with.

Notably, all agencies involved with preparation of curricula prescription of textbooks and organisation of educational processes will have to evince awareness towards women's issues. University/College Departments of Women's Studies, appropriate voluntary agencies, women's groups, etc. should be involved in giving a new perspective to the various issues of content and processes of education.

Women's universities and women's centres in colleges need to take an active role in women's development and in influencing the attitudes of future generations. Facilities for part-time self-study and correspondence courses should be provided on a large scale to enable girls who are not in a position to join higher educational institutions on a regular basis, to continue their studies. In addition to courses leading to degree/diploma, short courses in specific subjects through summer school sessions, and ad hoc programmes like seminars, workshops etc., should be organised for working women with a view to upgrading their knowledge and skills, not necessarily leading to degrees.

Integrated learning programmes for women are recommended which will not only lay emphasis on literacy but on empowering women through awareness building on social issues, bringing about attitudinal change, promoting skill training for employment, providing information on health care, nutrition and hygiene as well as on legal rights. Such programmes are beginning and must continue to be designed and structured so as to be relevant for the vast majority of rural women.

The revised scheme linked to ICDS known as the 'Women's Integrated Learning for Life', should be introduced as an integral part of the non-formal education system. Entrepreneurship development programmes should be organised separately for education of women in the age-group 18-30 years, with a minimum of matriculation level of education.

The objective of such training should be to (i) Make them aware of the various opportunities for self-employment; (ii) Motivate them to take up self-employment; (iii) Impart needed skills and training; (iv) Promote motivation for achievement among them; and (v) Create access to resources such as capital credit etc.

Notably, a large number of girls cannot participate in whole-day education programmes. Provision of non-formal and part-time programmes, with flexible school hours and sensitivity to the agricultural cycle are, of particular importance. In addition to the primary and upper primary stage, distance learning opportunities need to be provided at secondary and higher secondary level.

Adult education will have to be composed of three inter-related stands aimed at:

(i) Continuous flow of new information especially to rural and tribal areas, particularly to inculcate positive attitudes towards women;

(ii) Continuous training of the people in the use of modern tools and methods of production; and

(iii) Acquisition of permanent reading and computation skills.

The following from the above, three types of programmes may be offered to the learner;

(i) Information and literacy;

(ii) Information and training in new technology and literacy;

(iii) Information and training in new technology with or without literacy. Continuous information flows relating to human affairs, gender relations and the use of science and technology for betterment of life would be the common factor in all the three programmes.

Rapid strides in the development of technologies and tools for the reduction in women's drudgery and easy access to work places, water and fuel supply, child care, health services and population control can contribute significantly to the success of learning programmes for women. Women's literacy programmes would succeed better if they centre around women's concerns and also provide opportunities of recreation and sharing of experiences.

District plans should be prepared keeping in view literacy requirements of the learners, identifying agencies which can take up such programmes in districts.

All women working in industries or employed elsewhere should be made literate by the employers by allotting time from the working hours for their education. Place of teaching, teachers and teaching material should be arranged by them. Necessary legislation to this effect may be enacted. At least 50 per cent seats in pre-service courses in all teachers training institutions should be reserved for women. Spatial planning to ensure that women from rural areas are selected as teachers is essential. Provision of composite teacher training courses for women who have had insufficient education to improve their educational qualifications along with their training, should be made.

The existing Integrated Rural Development Programme, National Rural Employment Programme, Development of Women and Children in Rural Areas, Training of Youth in Self-Employment Programme, Integrated Child Development Programmes etc. should have a component of literacy for their women beneficiaries. Training should be provided to the functionaries of various development departments by the Directorate of Education in the States. The State Resources Centres should produce suitable learning material for women on a priority basis. Literature for neo-literate should be suitably devised by experts, keeping in view the needs of different groups of learners. Decentralisation is the key to the successful application of the strategies outlined above. In this decentralised approach, the village cluster or the block level is seen as most appropriate for the delivery of programmes.

It is, therefore, necessary that the block is allocated a flexible budget so as to make funds available to village clusters/villages for innovative educational activities and for equalisation of educational opportunity. An overall coordination of health, welfare and educational inputs would be most desirable.

This would entail (a) Convergent policies in these sectors; (b) Coordination of delivery mechanisms, and (c) Pooling of allocations.

The strategies spelt out in the National Policy of Education, 1986, the Programme of Action for its implementation and the National Literacy Mission and the successful achievement of the goals imposed in these documents, would be important for improvement in the status of women.

WOMEN DEVELOPMENT AND EDUCATIONAL COMMUNICATION

The basic question that has dominated research and the development of contemporary theory in the study of mass media can be summed up in simple terms—namely, "What has been their affect? That is, how have the mass media influenced us, as individuals in terms of persuading us to believe in new political ideologies, to vote for a particular party, to purchase more goods, to alter or abandon our cultural tastes, to reduce or strengthen our prejudices, to commit acts of crime, or to adopt an innovation? Even though from time to time attention his been given to some other aspect of the media, for example, to the nature of the communicator, the structure of media content, or the nature of audiences, the ultimate purpose was to see how variations in these factors have influenced the kinds of responses that have resulted from exposure to the media. Propositions concerning the impact of the media on individuals and groups have undergone progressive change. This change, has for the most part been a continuous and cumulative discovery of important intervening processes between media and mass, that is between the stimulus and the response.

The Individual Differences Theory

The basic proposition of this theory is that different people view or perceive particular events from quite different perspectives. The experimental study of human perception had revealed that the individual's values, needs beliefs, and attitudes played an influential role in determining how he selected stimuli from the environment and the way/ he attributed meaning to those stimuli within his required frames of reference once they came to his attention. Perception differed from one person to another according to the nature of his personality structure. So it became clear that the audience of a given medium was not a monolithic collectivity that attended uniformly to whatever content was direct toward it.

The principle of selective/attention and perception was formulated as a fundamental proposition regarding the communication behaviour of the ordinary person. It was not difficult to show that different types of people in an audience selected and interpreted mass communication content in widely variant ways. From the multiplicity of available content, the member of the audience selectively attended to massages, particularly if they were related to his interests, and consistent with his attitudes and beliefs. His response to such messages was modified by his psychological make-up.

This general idea is called the individual differences theory of mass communication. When communication "effects" are a focus of research attention, the assumption that the media are in some way "causes" of those effects is a natural one. Even if it is granted that intervening processes of somesome sort can soften or otherwise modify this relationship, the underlying cause-effect conceptualisation is not different, only more complicated. The individual difference theory of mass communication implies that media messages contain particular stimulus attributes that have differential interaction with personality characteristics of members of the audience. Since there are individual differences in personality characteristics among such members, it is natural to assume that there will be variations in effect which correspond to such individual differences. However, by holding constant the mediating influence of personality variables (that by considering people with similar personality characteristics), such a theory would still predict uniformity of response to a given message.

The Psycho-Dynamic Model of the Persuasion Process

The individual differences theory was and remains an important basic theory of mass communication effect. This conception has had a particular impact upon the advertising world and it has been the principle set of assumptions underlying a considerable number of social-psychological studies of the persuasion process that have accumulated in recent years. Persuasion is only one possible "effect" among many, but one upon which great attention has been focused. It has been assumed that an effective persuasive message is one which has properties capable of altering the psychological functioning of the individual in such a way that he will respond overtly in modes desired or suggested by the communicator.

That is, it has been assumed that the key to persuasion lies in modifying the internal psychological structure of the individual so that the psychodynamic relationship between latent internal processes and manifest overt behaviour will lead to acts intended by the persuader. A common example would be an attempt to promote the purchase of a patent medicine (overt action) by instilling a fear of poor health or continued suffering (psychological process).

The Social Categories Theory

Parallel with and sometimes overlapping the individual differences theory is the social categories theory. The latter assumes that there are broad collectives, aggregates, or social categories whose behaviour in the face of a given set of stimuli is more or less uniform. Such characteristics as age, sex, income level, educational attainment, rural-urban residence, or religious affiliation provide examples. Fashion magazines are not often bought by males; fishing magazines are seldom read by females.

In fact, knowledge of several very simple variables—age, sex and education—provides a reasonably accurate guide to the type of communication content a given individual will or will not select from available media. The basic assumption of this theory is that in spite of the heterogeneity of modern society, people who have a number of similar characteristics will have similar mass communication thought ways. These similar modes of orientation and behaviour will relate them to the mass media in a fairly uniform way, and they will respond to it in roughly equal ways.

The social categories theory is less an explanatory formulation than a kind of descriptive formula, but insofar as it can serve as a basis for rough prediction and as a guide for research it has functioned as a crude theory in the study of communication. While the individual differences theory presented a view of the communication process more consistent with findings in general psychology, the social categories theory was consistent with the more general sociological theories. Both take into account the idea that variations in stimulus factors, in media in content, as well as in audience, can have far reaching influence on the effects achieved by mass communication.

In fact, Lasswell summed up precisely these two theories and the situational variables related to them, when he stated that "A convenient way to describe an act of communication is to answer the following question; who, says what, in which channel to whom, with what affect? While these two theories remain useful, there have been further additions to the set of social and psychological variables intervening between media stimuli and audience response.

The Social Relationships Theory

The image of society in the minds of most students of communication, until very recently, was of atomised individuals connected with the mass media, but not with one another, and little thought was given to the relationships implied thereby to more informal relationships.

This theory states that informal social relationships play a significant role in modifying the manner in which a given individual will act upon a message which comes to his attention via the mass media. This theory began to suggest that there was a kind of movement of information through two basic stages. First, information moved from the media to relatively well-informed individuals who attended to mass communications first hand. Second, it moved from those persons through interpersonal channels to individuals who had less direct exposure to media and who depended on others for their information. This kind of communication process was termed the two-step flow of communication. Those individuals who were more in contact with the media were called opinion leaders. These opinion leaders were not only passing on information, but they were passing on their interpretations of the content. This kind of *personal influence* became immediately recognised as a kind of response to that message. Thus, contemporary theories of mass communication recognise not only the importance of individual psychological differences and the role of social categories in shaping the responses people make to the media, but the influence of informal group ties has also become increasingly clear.

The Sociocultural Model of the Persuasion Process

A socio-cultural model of the persuasion process follows from the idea that media effects in general are influenced by the social interactions a group member has with his follows. As his been suggested, social and cultural variables play a part in the diffusion of new products, beliefs and attitudes.

A substantial body of behaviour research and theory suggests that socio-cultural variables are important sources of *definitions for appropriate behaviour* that occurs within groups, and for interpretations of realities for the person. The research also indicates the way in which such variables as organisational membership, work roles, reference groups, cultural norms, and primary group norms can play a part in shaping and channelling overt action in ways that are to some extent unifluenced by internal psychological redispositions. To explain, predict, or manipulate individual's behaviour, reference must be made to the social norms and culturally defined values, in order that it can be effectively understood. A persuasion model suggested from these considerations is based upon the assumption that new definitions can be given (for instance by changing cultural norm) to socio-cultural processes in groups with the use of mass media. If individuals to be persuaded are members of these groups, it may by this means be possible to give new directions to their overt actions somewhat independently of their psychological predispositions.

It must be stressed that persuasion is not the only effect that mass communication can have. It is one among many. The socio-cultural model of persuasion, for this reason, flows from and is corollary to the more general social relationships theory of mass communication effects.

3

Women As Human Resource

> "Tradition is not a tomb in which to hide from progress. It is rich ground well-tilled and warm with the sunshine of hope fro an even greater future. Into it we drop the seeds of our aspiration for a better world and from it they grow strong and well-nourished and bear fruit and become new traditions to nourish others as time passed."
>
> —*Philip Ogilivie*

Women constitute a vast human resource potential. Here in this chapter we will describe women resource development in detail.

First it is pertinent to note that the status of women in India is somewhat different from those of Western countries. Women have often been considered a weaker section of Indian society. However, in the past few decades much attention is paid towards women's problems all over the world. The equality of status of women with man has become an important and burning issue at the political and social levels.

A growing concern was evident during the recent past to study various aspects of women life and a number of researches have offered significant and valuable knowledge about Indian women. The contribution of women in many spheres like economic, technological, entrepreneurship, and organisation and management was minimal and was not acknowledged. Even today the situation is not very promising.

With the changing times efforts have been made to optimise industrial productivity and technological innovations have been introduced to minimise costs and efforts. Various technologies and processes have become costly and obsolete with each innovation.

The technological advances have brought in a variety of changes in the life- style and working patterns of individuals which demand more attention and adaptation of the changing environment both in social and work life.

It is pertinent to note that concern for women development has been witnessed in the past decades and efforts for their development in various spheres have been examined with care. Socio-economic, political and legal changes necessary for equation the status of women at par with men have been activated. Women have been considered equal partners in national development. Several development programmes, specially designed for women to play their role in the national mainstream, have been implemented. Contribution of women in the area of rural development and agriculture, supportive services like fuel and fodder, water and political and social participation have now been recognised.

It has been envisaged to encompass these areas into governmental efforts for their development efforts and these efforts aim to provide more facilities in the areas of education, housing, creche/day care services, health and family welfare, legislation, decision-making, media and communication, and voluntary action. The percentage increase in employment of women has not been founded less than that of males. Organised sector (which consists of public sector and non-agricultural private sector) absorbs less than one-eighth of the actual work force of the country. Of this women's employment in the organised sector grew from 19.30 lakhs in 1971 to an estimated 33.41 lakhs in 1986. The main source of data on women labour force are available from the NSSO Census and other surveys (e.g., employment exchange, EMI etc.).

The finding of NSSO survey exhibited that women employment has been steadily going up in rural India. In urban India also women employment went up from 1972-73 to 1977-78 and was still higher in 1983. These figures are clearly indicative of an increasing trend of women's employment. It is noticed that a majority of working women are found in the rural and urban sector. National Commission of Self-Employed Women reported that 94 per cent of total female workforce operates within highly exploited unorganised sector. Low pay, long hours of work, low productivity skills and lack of job security are predominantly operating factors. A large share of employment in the rural unorganised sector is of women. Women mostly in employment in this sector are working in agriculture, social and agro-forestry, khadi and village industries, handloom, handicrafts and sericulture.

In urban areas a large number of women are employed as unskilled labour in building construction industry besides other occupations. The construction labours are engaged on casual (daily of piece rates) basis but many of them have to their credit long years of experience in construction work. The exploitation of these workers begains with their methods of recruitment. These female labourers benefit the contractor and sub-contractors to keep profit margins high. Domestic work offers another main avenue to women and girls for employment. These workers like others in the unorganised sector have remained grossly neglected to get even a fraction of benefits from governmental programmes and schemes for women. This sector especially is the most unregulated and disorganised.

As estimate reported in Sanrakshana (1987) for the period 1977-78 has given high figures of females as opposed to male domestic workers (i.e., 1.68 million vs 0.62 respectively). The working hours and other conditions of work for women are not encouraging. They do not get either an alternative employment or sill training and education of any kind. The National Commission on self-employed Women and Women in the Informal sector has identified women workers in the primary sector in mining, tobacco and beedi work, handicraft and garment, hendlooms, women vendors and hawkers, construction workers and domestic workers. A study worth mention was conducted by Mathur (1989). He has, in his study on Quality of Work Life of Women Construction Workers, stressed on the poor quality of work life of women in building construction industry and has discussed about burden of this industry on the poor women who suffer due to lack of permanent employment, proper living conditions, general awareness of urban life-style, proper opportunities for acquiring minimum education and training of construction skills and other related factors.

Mathur (1989) has offered a number of valuable suggestions requiring adequate attention on women working in this sector. Technological modernisation has shrinked scope for women employment and has further eliminated various traditional employment activities. Investment outlays on unorganised sector (in agriculture, dairying, fisheries, small animal husbandry, Khadi and village industries, handicrafts, sericulture and handlooms) have been placed high priority, and several governmental programmes exist to boost the productivity, most endeavours are focussed on men and male producer establishments.

Even these programmes have been implemented by male bureaucrats and extension education workers. Women are considered indirect beneficiaries through male members of their households and are not participants and the target groups. Most of the jobs are low paid that are performed by women. Women are also been gradually displaced from these occupations in unorganized and informal sectors.

As a result of heirarchical pattern of land ownership structural problems have arisen in the rural unorganised sector; the nature of land relations and division of labour on the basis of sex and the credit system also pose serious problems so far as women are concerned. The economically weaker sections and particularly women are put to disadvantage owing to a strong class-caste relationship. The overall situation in rural and urban unorganised sectors particularly in the primary sector and informal sector demand attention as these sectors have been left neglected to a large extent.

In fact, special efforts are, therefore, required to provide facilities and services so as to enable them to cater to their lower order needs (food, shelter, clothes) adequately. Presently even these basic needs are not adequate. Intensive efforts are needed to improve quality of life and working conditions for women employed in these sectors.

There is lack of permanent employment, proper living conditions, general awareness of life-style and proper opportunities for acquiring minimum education and training of requisite work skills. There is also serious lack or organisation and management in unorganised informal sectors. Systematic approaches, strategies, programmes and intensive efforts are required to facilitate the governmental policies for focuss on women essentially. Strategies and programmes in general have led nowhere near the envisaged results so far as women are concerned. Therefore in order to facilitate systematic human resource development a strategy is required which would focus essentially on women development.

Three levels of training for women has been recommended in National Perspective Plan for Women (1988-2000 A.D.) (a) grass-root level; (b) middle level; and (c) policy and planning level. The training strategy should encompass five principal components, viz., organisational and extension training, skill training, management and entrepreneurial training, sensitisation of administrators/ implementors to women in development issues and training of trainers.

(1) Organisational and Extension Training

Organisational and extension training component would be aimed to be geared to functionaries, catalysts, extension workers at the grass-root level, middle and supervisory level personnel, teachers, organizers of cooperatives etc. The objectives of this training would also be the conscientisation on legislation, environmental health, nutrition and sanitation, education, functional literacy, para legal training and related aspects. Effective group mobilisation, communications skills needed for organisation and management would be emphasised in the training programmes alongwith functional knowledge. Particular attention would be paid to the attitudinal/behavioural component which is essentially an important objective of any training program. This would facilitate participants in reaching the programmes for women at the grass-root level.

2. Skill Training

Skill training would be planned with special emphasis on the nine major sectors of women's employment i.e., agriculture, dairying, fisheries, small animal husbandry, Khadi and Village industries, handlooms, handicrafts, sericulture and social forestry. The modules of training would be planned with the objective of upgrading existing skills in these areas as also training of women in appropriate technologies. It would be aimed at programme beneficiaries, catalysts/functionaries, and extension and supervisory workers. The skills need to be imparted on wide scale to rural women in order to encourage them to achieve household sufficiency and supplementary income. Such training programmes would also include skill training in urban/ modern sector with regard to assembly, manufacturing and processing for larger industries and small scale firms. Employability for women would be increased in the organised sector as the employment conditions in the unorganised sector indicate need for a shift in the occupational structure. Necessary care would be taken in development of skills to ensure that the training imparted does not push women into sectors where mobility is limited, wages are low, health hazards are high and worker benefits are not enforced.

3. Management Training

Management training would include project formulation, monitoring, evaluation, information systems, credit/marketing management, and other skills required toe administer and manage projects as well as supervisory and entrepreneurial skills. This training would be imparted with the help of technical institutes (ITIs, Polytechniques etc.) where special courses for training of women workers and entrepreneurs could be started. In conducting such courses, Banks, voluntary organisations and private and public sector industries could be effectively utilised to help formulate viable entrepreneurial projects for trainees. There are different approaches to analyses the Management Development (MD) training programmes. Different psychological approaches to behaviour have led to appreciate importance of M.D. training and these approaches have suggested that individual differences play an important role and, therefore, individual differences should not be overlooked.

Emphasis on integrated development of personality of trainee is one of the major objectives of most of the MD training programmes today. A well conceived MD training programme, therefore, has to be aware of generality of behavioural characteristics. The training programme thus planned have been considered successful in achieving the objectives of optimum HRD. The management training for women, as envisaged to be organised by the ITIs, polytechniques. etc. has to take into consideration the fact that unless expert management trainers impart training under the conducive training conditions such a training as thought of for the women would be of little us to them.

The specific skill development training and management development training are different types of training, basic difference is that on one hand there is development of specific worker skills and on the other skills to management of man and material resources are involved. For the management training a minimum understanding level and qualifications are required.

It is pertinent here to mention that this type of training would be useful for urban/modernised sector only. Workers of rural unorganised sector and informal and primary sector would not be benefited by such training programmes.

4. Sensitisation of Administrators/Implementors

This type of training would seek to achieve sensitisation of bureaucrats to the critical need to integrate women in development. The objective of such training will be to develop appropriate attitudes and knowledge for planning, monitoring, implementing programmes and policies for women. Such training programmes of the Department of Personnel as well as other governmental and non-governmental agencies. Particular emphasis in this category of training must be to train officers in charge of enforcement machineries at the Central and State levels, workers of quasi-governmental bodies, and voluntary agencies.

The Womens Division at NIPCCD has already undertaken sensitisation programmes for policy officers/ judiciary to the issue of crimes against women.

5. Training of Trainers

Besides training trainers within the existing institutions and infrastructures, special efforts should be made to train rural women as organisers and instructors in different sectors and trade so that they could/train more women and achieve a multiple-effect.

In view of the above analysis and recommendations the core group on National Perspective Plan of women has suggested that a National Resource Centre of Women may be set up in order to play an important role in coordinating/ interventionist role and identify and strengthen existing governmental and non-governmental agencies to carry out training policy and programme research alongwith information dissemination.

Remarkably, setting up of Resource Organisation is important in view of the status of women with special reference to employed women in different sectors. Training has been recognised as an important strategy to HRD and women-oriented training in particular needs focus of attention. Voluntary agencies may come forward in order to bring about systematic HRD with special emphasis on women's development as human resources.

Their role in developmental efforts would substantiate the existing governmental efforts. Nonetheless governmental role is crucial and if an systematic HRD is the objective for national development, development of women as human resources is a must. Training is one of the main mechanisms for HRD therefore due emphasis on evolving women- oriented and need based training programmes should be the first important step.

Infact, the existing knowledge on management and training as a means of Organisational Development and HRD may be of immense use in order to systematically plan and organise training for development. One of the concepts related to the goal of HRD in organisations is concept of quality of work life (QWL). The QWL has been defined as the degree to which members of a work organisation are able to satisfy important personal needs through their experiences in the organisations. The definition implies that the QWL can be assured by measures of need importance and need satisfaction.

The QWl thus refers to the interaction between individual employees and their organisations. The needs of employees for material rewards and changes to learn and grow must somehow be meshed with the needs of the organisation for attaining goal of productivity, creativity, loyalty and high performance.

The QWL also relates to the needs of individuals. There is, therefore, necessity to apply needs analysis to gain knowledge about individuals and organisational needs so that both may be meshed together for growth and development of employees as well as organisation.

Brinkerhoff (1986) has emphasised on expanding needs analysis by redefining the function of needs analysis to realise organisational goals. Mager and Pipe (1970) and Rummler (1976) have mentioned that in order to avoid providing training to meet non-training problems needs analysis has been constructed as a "Problem solving" effort. It is necessary to recognise the value component of need for expanded understanding of needs analysis. When it is said that something is needed means that it is necessary or useful in serving some value purpose e.g. money itself meets no need but has utility in gaining things that are valued.

Similarly, training itself provides no outcome that has intrinsic value. The value of training outcomes may be established only relative to the degree that they serve, or are useful for achieving something that the organisation values.

Thus, needs analysis must establish the potential value of training effort to the organisation, and need - analysis must answer basic questions like (a) what good, if any, can training do? and (b) How valuable, relative to other possible "goods", it is good that training do?

HRD should concern itself with what is right or what is wrong. Use of systems to describe and develop human resources has been used during the past few years. Systems provide a logical and thorough approach. In HRD, systems method has been utilised in the design of instructional systems so as to meet the training needs of groups. Use of systems approach would facilitate to find out specific objectives of a training programme (Kumar, 1987).

These approaches, if applied, would bring about the desirable seriousness of efforts for HRD with particular emphasis on women development which is to be of focal importance for national development plans.

It is pertinent to note that in the context of development of training programmes and modules for training of women the needs analysis approach would be useful. Thorough micro-level needs analysis would reveal real training needs which, in turn would facilitate development of training programmes specific to the felt needs for training of beneficiaries intended to be trained. Systems approach may be applied at a little later stage when the process of training would be started which would help in identifying content of training modules at micro-level in order to make training efforts effective and useful for/trainee participants.

REFEREMCES

Brinkerhoff, Robert O. (1986). Brinkerhoff, Robert O.: *Expanding Needs Analysis, Training and Development Journal. American Society for Training and Development* (ASID) Inc., Alexendria, Va., February, 1964-65.

Kumar, Salil (1987). Psychological Correlates of Management Development Training Programmes. Doctoral Thesis (Unpublished,) IIT Delhi, New Delhi.

Kumar, Salil: Psychological Correlates of Management Development Training Programmes. Doctoral Thesis (Unpublished,) IIT Delhi, New Delhi, 1987.

Mager, R.F. and Pipe, P. (1989). *Analyzing performance problems.* Palo Alto. California; Fearon Publishers.

Mager, R.F. and Pipe, P.: Analyzing performance problems. Palo Alto. California; Fearon Publishers, 1989.

Mathur, R.N. (1989). Quality of Working Life of Women Construction Workers, Commonwealth Publishers, New Delhi.

Mathur, R.N.: Quality of Working Life of Women Construction Workers, Commonwealth Publishers, New Delhi, 1989.

Rummler, G.A.: The performance audit. Training and Development Handbook (2nd ed.), McGraw Hill, N.Y., 1976.: Expanding Needs Analysis, Training and Development Journal. American Society for Training and Development (ASID) Inc., Alexendria, Va., February, 1964-65.

Rummler, G.A.: The performance audit. Training and Development Handbook (2nd ed.), McGraw Hill, N.Y., 1976.

4

University Education Commission on Women

> "The power of words is immense. A well-chosen word has often sufficed to stop a flying army, to change defeat into victory, and to save an empire."
>
> —*Emile de Girardin*

Women's education was a neglected factor in India. To improve their condition concerted efforts were made by the Government soon after attaining the Independence.

Here in this chapter we will describe salient features of Dr. Radhakrishnan Commission's Report pertaining to the women education in India.

CHAPTER II
THE AIMS OF UNIVERSITY EDUCATION

Universities as the Organs of Civilisation

He indeed must be blind who does not see that, mightly as are the political changes, far deeper are the fundamental questions which will be decided by what happens in the universities. Everything is being brought to the test of reason, venerable theologies, ancient political institutions, time-honoured social arrangements, a thousand things which a generation age looked as fixed as the hills. If India is to confront the confusion of out time, she must turn for guidance, not to those who are lost in the mere exigencies of the passing hour, but to her men of letters and men of science, to her poets and artists, to her discoverers and inventors. These intellectual pioneers of civilisation are to be found and trained in the universities, which are the sanctuaries of the inner life of the nation.

In simpler conditions of life, in primitive societies, the leader can follow the urge of his instinct and take us to the scene of his vision. In the complex organisation of modern life, any reform requires careful thought and planning. Our leaders must be capable of intellectual analysis and imaginative insight.

Intellectual Adventure

We must give up the fatal obsession of the perfection of the past, that greatness is not to be attained in the present, that everything is already worked out and all that remains for the future ages of the world is pedantic imitation of the past. When we are hypnotised by our own past achievements, when all our effort is to repeat a past success, we become fetish worshippers. If our cultural life is to retain its dynamism, it must give up idolatory of the past and strive to realise new dreams.

We should think with the young men in the Latin poem that nothing is down while anything remaining to do. All that man has yet done is very little compared to what he is destined to achieve. The present which moves backwards and forwards, which is a summary of the past and a prophecy of the future, is hallowed ground and we who tread on it should face it with the quality of reverence and the spirit of adventure. Universities are the homes of intellectual adventure.

An Integrated Way of Life

A life of strenuous for human betterment is not possible, if we are not persuaded that life has a meaning. Many of our popular writers today seem to be possessed by the one desire to escape from the world of meaning and teach us the essential purposelessness of life. They make us believe, with a good deal of cleverness and sophistry, that life is infinitely complicated and totally inexplicable. Many of our students are taught to assume that free-will and personal responsibility are illusions, that human beings are conditioned almost wholly by their physical make-up and the society in which they live, and that the only sense that the religious statements make is it emotional and subjective.

This is a generation which knows to doubt but not to admire, much less to believe. This aimlessness, this indifference to basic issues, is to no small extent, responsible for the decline of standards, for the fading of ideals, for the defeat of human endeavour. The purpose of all education, it is admitted by thinkers of East and West, is to provide a coherent picture of the universe and an integrated way of life. We must obtain through it a sense of perspective, a synoptic vision, a samanvays of the different items of knowledge.

Man cannot live by a mass of disconnected information. He has a passion for an ordered intellectual vision of the connections of things. Life is one in all its varied manifestations. We may study the factual relations of the different manifestations but we must have knowledge of life as a whole.

It cannot be a collection of distracting scraps, but should be a harmony of patterns. The subjects we study must be taught as parts of a curriculum.

Wisdom and Knowledge

Our ancient teachers tried to teach subjects and impart wisdom. Their local wisdom (irfan) along with knowledge (ilam), jnanam vijnanam-sahitam. We cannot be wise without some basis of knowledge though we may easily acquire knowledge and remain devoid of wisdom. To use the words of the Upanishad, we may be the knowers of texts (mantravit) and not knowers of self (atmavit). Plato distinguishes between factual information and understanding. No amount of factual information would make ordinary men into educated or "virtuous" men unless something is a awakened in them, an innate ability to live the lief of the soul.

> Where is the wisdom we have lost in knowledge?
> Where is the knowledge we have lost in information?
> The cycles of heaven in twenty centuries?
> Bring us further from God and nearer to the dust.

The strength of the new "faiths" among intellectuals is apartly due to their to explain the universe. By professing to interpret all human activity in terms of a single thesis, they give to the modern educated men a sense of assurance and certainty formerly provided by religion. Since education is both a training of minds and a training of souls, it should give both knowledge and wisdom.

Aims of the Social Order

We must have a conception of the social order for which we are educating our youth. We know that Hitler did in six years with the German youth. The Russians are clear in their minds about the kind of society for which they are educating and the qualities required in their citizens. They tried to remake man in a new image. Our educational system must find its guiding principle in the aims of the social order for which it prepares, in the nature of the civilisation it hopes it build. Unless we know whether we are tending, we cannot decides what we should do and how we should do it. Societies like men need a clear purpose to keep them at stable in a world of bewildering change.

The outlines of the social philosophy which should govern all our institutions, educational as well as economic and political, are indicated in the preamble to our Draft Constitution, it reads:

> We the People of India, having solemnly resolved to constitute India to a Sovereign Democratic Republic and to secure to all its citizens;
>
> Justice, social, economic and political;
>
> Liberty of status and opportunity; and to promote among them all Fraternity, assuming the dignity of the individual and the unity of the Nation;
>
> In Our Constituent Assembly this.................
>
> of.................
>
> (..... day of August, 1949 A.D.) do

Hereby Adopt, Enact and Give to Ourselves this Constitution.

We are engaged in a quest for democracy though the realisation of justice, liberty, equality and fraternity.

The Need for Culture

What holds a society together and gives the individual balance and perspective, is the possession of culture. Culture is intellectual alertness, receptiveness, to beauty, human feeling, social enthusiasm.

As the result of the vest expansion of the area of knowledge and the diversification of its content, the aim of teaching has become almost exclusively specialisation. It is the normal feature in professional colleges. Even in colleges for liberal arts and sciences, the tendency is to specialise and prepare for advanced study in one or the other special field. If society is not to disintegrate into an aggregate of individual specialists, we should endow the youth with a central core of values, transmit to them a cultural heritage. It alone can serve as a cohesive force in a society which is getting splintered by over-specialisation. It will confer a unity and consistency of aim on specialised vocational courses and make for a more abundant personal life and a freer social order.

The Un-Indian Character of Education

One of the serious complaint against the system of education which has prevailed in this country for over a century is that it neglected India's past, that it did not provide the Indian students with a knowledge of their own culture. It has produced in some cases the feeling that we are without roots, in others, what is worse that our roots bind us to a world very different from that which surrounds us.

A British historian of Indian education observes: "our education has done far less for Indian Culture than for the material and political progress of India. She looks to our Schools and Colleges for equipment in the struggle for existence; for the secret of happy living, vivendi causae, she looks elsewhere".

Cultural Unity of India

Nations are not made chiefly by traders and politicians. They are made by artists and thinkers, saints and philosophers. National unity and progress require a deeper foundation than political and economic arrangements. It is the life of spirit that has shaped and unified our collective existence and has been the real bond of oneness among the Indian people. After centuries of stress and conflict India has gradually evolved a common civilisation, a collective consciousness which embraces wide varieties of temperament, tradition, ways of thought and belief.

Our people belong to different provinces, speak their own language, reserves their own habits and customs. There are sharp differences of temper, tradition and dialect. Despite all these there is a fundamental unity which binds the people together as members of one society with the same cultural loyalities.

Indian culture is like a palimpsest in which new characters do not entirely efface the old. In a single social pattern fragments of different ages are brought together. It would be impossible to think of an India where no Moghuls ruled, where no Taj was built, where no Macaulay wrote his Minute on education.

Indian culture is like a living organism growing in richness and content. Primitive cultures are marked by extreme conservatism where social groups follow the same path of custom and convention with irrational persistence. Living cultures are dynamic and maintain their cultural concern by a continuous effort of individual and social discipline.

Conflict in India's Soul

Two contradictory impulses have attracted Indian intellectuals. One is a jealous pride in Indian genius and tradition wholly distinct from those of the West. The other is the no less jealous desire to profit by the example of the West.

A revolutionary period is not generally inclined to respect the wisdom of the past, but to cultivate this disrespect would be to forgo out spiritual heritage. There are treasures of spirit which may not be of any conceivable use in the struggle for material comfort, but if we are to be qualified to assist or resist the dominant tendencies of our age, we cannot afford to ignore the standards and ideals built by the austerily and abnegation of our ancestors across the centuries. The chief course of spiritual nourishment for any people must be its own past perpectually rediscovered and renewed. A society without a knowledge of the past which has made it would be lacking in depth and dignity.

Critical Study of the Past

This is not to romanticise the past filling the gaps of memory from the resources of imagination. India has suffered on account of her great weaknesses, her spirit of reaction and narrow-mindedness. We must be critical and selective and use the past to illuminate the present. We should not blindly give up the great values of our past nor should we cling to beliefs simply because they are ancient. We should accept so much of ancient thought as is sympathetic to us.

Even in the darkest days of degradation, the light of India's culture never failed. It may have flickered but it was never extinguished. There were loving hands which cherished and tended it. Today it is burning with a renewed glow. If it is to become a consuming flame, we must became aware of its past-greatness and its contemporary value.

CHAPTER IV
STANDARDS OF TEACHING

Causes of Low Standards, Low Percentage of Passes, and Suggested Measures of Reform

There are several causes which contribute to the low average quality of our graduates and the low percentage of passes at the B.A. and the B.Sc. Examinations, but principal ones are the following:

Overcrowding in Colleges

During the last 10 to 15 years there has been a growing pressure of an increase in the number of admissions at the universities, but unfortunately, this wide and eager demand for university education is not proportional to the capacity to profit from such an education. The size of a college or a teaching university is determined by the number of students who can be accepted without a lowering of standards. Whatever may be done, in a burst of public enthusiasm. to expand university education, nothing should be allowed to lower the quality of work at the universities, and size, beyond a certain point, undeniably lowers the quality. A college or a university is like a living cell; once it reaches a certain size, it must either divide or die. The admission or a large number of students in response to popular demand without the necessary staff, class-room and hostel accommodation and equipment has made it impossible for most colleges and universities to give full education to their inflated undergraduate population. This factor, more than any other, has undoubtedly been responsible for the lowering of our standards. To quote Abraham Flexner, "bigness is almost necessarily fatal to greatness".

Resulting Evils

Some of the colleges we have visited have on their rolls five to ten times the number of students they could properly educate. They have neither adequate class-room space nor laboratory accommodation. The staff is miserably paid and we found that several teachers lectured at two or three colleges to eke out a living wage. In one of the colleges the management was saving 1.75 lacs a year on the running expenses of the college. This is an extreme case but we have found that with notable exceptions, there is a widespread tendency in colleges and universities, specially private colleges, to increase their enrolment in order to augment their fee income.

One of the harmful results of the large number of the average low quality of undergraduates in the first degree classes is that the abler and more capable students suffer; they fail to get the educational opportunities they deserve. Teachers have to teach down to the level of the average; in justice to the majority they are unable to raise questions or employ methods designed to call forth mental effort from those students who are capable of being highly trained; consequently they more promising are kept back by the less intelligent and there is much waste of good material.

Reduction of Numbers Recommended

Every college in an affiliating university and every teaching university should deliberately fix a maximum limit to the number of students it admits every year. This maximum limit will vary according to the size of the building, the number of teachers, laboratory space, hotel accommodation, etc., but the limit must be fixed and adhered to, if the quality of education is to be raised. It is the duty of the affiliating universities to fix and to enforce these limits on their colleges, and for the teaching universities to fix these limits to maintain proper standards.

Limitation of Number of U.P. Universities and Colleges

We heard with satisfaction that at a recent meeting of the Vice-Chancellors of the universities in U.P., it was decided that the teaching universities of Lucknow and Allahabad should not have more than 3,000 students in their Arts and Science faculties. While degree colleges affiliated to the Agra University should not have more than 1,000 students. We commend this move to other universities and colleges. For the present, however, the maximum number of students in a affiliated college will have to be 1,500 for some years.

Working Days and Vocations

The number of actual working days in the year in most colleges and universities is insufficient. At one university the number was as low as 120, which meant that students and teachers worked only for one-third of the year. Further, on account of the large number of stray holidays during the session, the continuity of work is broken and consequently the total output of work by teachers and students remains low. While it is necessary to close the colleges and the universities at most places for ten weeks during the season of intense heat, we must make the best use of the remaining 42 weeks of the year. In American universities, most of which work on a two semester (term) basis, each semester consists of about 91 working days beside examination days during the year. Generally, the only holidays they have are 15 days of Christmas, one Thanks giving day, 10 days of spring recess and 13 to 14 weeks of summer vacation.

The following table gives the numbers of working days, besides examination days, at some of the American universities during the session 1948-49:

Harward working days	1 7 2
Pennsylvania working days	1 7 4
Michigan working days	1 8 2
Johns Hopkins working days	1 8 8
Vanderbit working days	2 1 6

Minimum of 180 Days, Exclusive of Examination Days

We recommend that the university session be divided into three more or less equal terms, each of 10 to 11 week's duration separated by two short vacations of two or three weeks each and one long vacation of ten to thirteen weeks. All casual holidays during the currency of each term should be severely curtailed. Every college and university should so arrange its sessional work as to ensure a minimum number of 180 working days, exclusive of examination days.

Maximum Utilisation of Working Days

Not only should there be an increase in the number of working days, but it is also necessary that each day should be utilised to its maximum. There are teachers and students who attend the university only for two to three periods (100 to 150 minutes) a day. While there are conscientious teachers who keep their lectures up-to-date by reading and research, there are quite a number of others who deliver the same lectures, prepared years previously, year after year. It is these latter who give a bad name to the profession of a university teacher and lead to the criticism that university teaching is soft job. At one of the universities we were told that every teacher has to be on duty at the university for 6 hour a day—he may either teach or work in the library or laboratory.

This may be repugnant to some of the teachers but there is no doubt that some kind of check is necessary for teachers who do not realise their obligation to engage in research and keep themselves up-to-date in their knowledge.

As of now (in 2010) the status of women's education has improved a lot. We have improved intake of women students in higher education. Similarly women are entering in all sorts of jobs in great number. But despite all these achievements the picture is not very bright. We have to go long to reach the goal of universal women literacy.

5

Women Resource Development: Institutional Efforts

Ever since Independence, the development of India has witnessed kaleidoscopic changes from time to time. In this context various programmes were introduced under different names starting from Community Development (CD) to Integrated Rural Development (IRD) and Area Development. During the Second, Third and Fourth Five- Year Plans programmes for and participation of women and children did not receive any fresh impetus and continued on the earlier lines. But programme launched during Fifth Five Year Plan recognised the importance of women and child development.

Thereafter, social welfare as a plan component has acquired great significance, as evidenced by its widening interface with Government and increasing participation by voluntary agencies. From the Fifth Plan onwards, emphasis has been on the promotion of preventive and developmental services. As a result, several programmes in the areas of women and child welfare, namely, nutrition, health, education and recreation for children have launched by the Government.

However, developmental efforts, through successive

Five Year Plans, have contributed a great deal towards commendable improvements in the women's status. Even the community development programme accorded an important role to the organisation of women, who constitute nearly half of our population, so that their participation in various rural development activities could be effectively ensured.

These organisations of women, known as *Mahila Mandals,* came to be established in a phased manner in different states. The Integrated Child Development Services Scheme was launched in 1975 and has attracted wide attention over the years. The need for involvement of functional groups at grassroot level in the implementation of ICDS scheme has been emphasised time and again at various forums.

There is a growing realisation that development and responsibility are closely interlinked and that there can be no development if people do not feel responsible and involve themselves in development process. Development of any sector could take place only if the people were effectively drawn into the planning and implementation of schemes. The system of centralised planning and employment of personnel from outside, could not yield the expected results. In the context of the rural sector, women's development also posed the same problem. How could rural women be made more responsible for their own development?

Earlier Gram Sevikas, Mukhya Sevikas, Health workers and teachers with their urban background were not keen on continuing service in rural areas; the low educational backgrounds of girls in rural areas made it difficult to find qualified personnel in the rural setting, the vastness of the rural sector made it possible to find trained personnel to meet the out reach expectation.

To face these challenges, it became clear that greater involvement on a voluntary basis, by local women was a 'sine quo non' for the development of child care programmes. During the period of the Third Five Year Plan, encouragement was given to the establishment of Mahila Mandals in an effort to develop responsibility among local women. The unpreparedness of local women to take up such responsibility as well as the apathy of the community a large in this regard have posed problems for the proper functioning in many Mahila Mandals. The contribution and involvement of women's organisation in national development has been considered vital due to their direct and first hand experience and knowledge of local needs, problems and resources of the grassroots.

Secondly, commitment and zeal of voluntary action is not considered effective as it is not bound by rigid bureaucratic systems and is more responsive to people. Thirdly, these organisations are observed to operate with greater flexibility and base their activities on felt needs. They often function more effectively than the government managed agencies in the field of women and child development. The rationale for involvement of Mahila Mandals/Women Groups in ICDS programme is quite clear. The programme suffer from multifarious constraints such as a low level of literacy, lack of access to resources and obstacles caused by the cultural and social customs and traditions. In a situation such as this, the role of Mahila Mandals/Women Groups in creating awareness among target groups is of immense importance.

As a result various ministries and departments have formulated programmes for the development of women and children. It was realised that the objectives of ICDS scheme could not be achieved without the active participation and leadership of the local community. Government functionaries, however, efficient and dedicated, can only provide some stimulus and act as a catalytic agent to train and release efforts for self-help of the people. This was particularly true of women who had been paralysed by generations of social oppression, and denial of basic rights. Even different government departments have also concluded that the proper agency for the success of programme would be a committee of local women.

The organisation of Mahila Mandals thus, become one of the objectives of the programme. The declared objective of community development is to enable rural women to organise themselves at the village level to assemble on a regular basis to learn from each other and from Workers appointed by government. The basic idea is to create opportunities for rural women to improve their status as house-wives and to take part in public affairs.

The department therefore, organises Mahila Mandals, imparts training facilities to their members and provide incentives/awards for performance. Mahila Mandals were organised in villages and blocks for promoting women's and children programmes. The Central Social Welfare Board and the State Social Welfare Advisory Boards also realised the importance of Mahila Mandals and after 1961 they were being given grants up to 75 per cent for running some programmes of the Board. They were also running some Welfare Extension Projects of the Board.

Even voluntary agencies like the Bhartiya Grameen Mahila Sangh have also established a large number of Mahila Mandals. In fact, steps have been taken to utilise the potential of the Mahila Mandals in implementing some selected programmes such as the Applied Nutrition Programme (ANP), the Integrated Child Development Services (ICDS) and Composite Programme for Women and Preschool Children. They are also being encouraged to take up production-oriented activities such as kitched gardening, poultry, fishery in addition to feeding demonstrations, propagation of family welfare and non-formal education programmes.

Two more schemes, namely, 'Incentive Awards of Mahila Mandals,' and 'Training of Associate Women Workers' were introduced in the Fourth Five-Year Plan. Under the former scheme Mandals showing good performance over an year were to be given cash awards for undertaking economic projects or activities. The latter scheme was designed to provide orientation to selected women having leadership qualities in organaising village women and assisting them in implementing various welfare programmes. A number of Mandals and women leaders have been benefited under these schemes.

During Fifth Five Year Plan, another scheme, 'Promotion of Voluntary Action' was initiated with a view to utilising the women's organisations in the implementation of various programmes meant for women and children. People's active participation and cooperation is the key to the success of a social and developmental programme like ICDS which is aimed at bringing about a change in the life of the people.

The factors considered crucial for strengthening and promoting ICDS services were skills of the workers, active participation of Mahila Mandal, existence of Coordination Committees, frequency of their meetings and the involvement of other local organisations.

However, question of central importance to the present study is to know the extent of contribution and involvement of Mahila Mandals and women groups in strengthening the ICDS scheme. The investigation is largely confined to the involvement and contribution of Mahila Mandals/women groups in different components of ICDS scheme.

The Scheme

It's pertinent to note that the Integrated Child Development Services was launched in 1975 for providing opportunities of physical and psychosocial development of children in the age-group 0-6 years through an integrated package of early childhood services.

These services include supplementary nutrition, immunisation, health check-up, referral services and treatment for minor illness for these children and expectant and nursing mothers, pre-school education for children in the age-group of 3 to 6 years and nutrition and health education for all women in the age-group 15 to 45 years. The services are provided through the ICDS projects located mostly at the block level. With its expansion in successive Five-Year Plans; ICDS is today a major programme of child development at the national level.

Objectives of ICDS

- to improve the nutritional and health status of children in the age-group 0 to 6 years;
- to lay the foundation for proper psychological, physical and social development of the child;
- to reduce the incidence of mortality, malnutrition and school dropout;
- to achieve effective coordination of policy and implementation amongst the various departments to promote child development; and
- to enhance the capability of the mother to look-after the child through proper nutrition and health education.

Remarkably, the objectives are sought to be achieved by delivery on integrated pack of early childhood services comprising supplementary nutrition, immunization, health check-up and referral services for children (0 to 6 years) and for expectant and nursing mothers, by providing health and nutrition education to mothers, and by imparting non-formal pre-school education to the children in the age-group 3 to 6 years.

The objectives of the scheme are implemented through the projects located mostly at the block level. Launched initially with 33 ICDS projects and 2nd October, 1975 on experimental basis in 22 states and Union Territory of Delhi, the scheme sanctioned 2424 projects and 210765 Anganwadi Centres by the end of June 1990.

In pursuance of the National Policy for Children the scheme of ICDS was launched in 33 projects on experimental basis in October, 1975. As the concept and the performance of the programme over the years had attracted wide attention, several studies have been conducted on the impact of services delivered through ICDS projects. The Planning Commission conducted a Baseline survey of the ICDs projects for the reference period of 1976-77 to find out the state of preparedness of these projects to deliver the services effectively and whether necessary infrastructural support was available for that.

The Repeat Round was undertaken of the projects for the reference period of 1977-78 to evaluate the extent of coverage of target population and the impact of the scheme on beneficiaries. A number of research studies on ICDS have concluded that the scheme by and large, has helped in improving the health and nutritional status of children and mothers in the target groups. It was concluded that the component of pre-school education was not correctly understood by the ICDS functionaries while health and nutrition education has not received adequate attention, and the community contribution and participation in the ICDS programme was negligible.

Lack of effective supervision of the programme at the Anganwadi level for functional coordination at different levels of the project and lack of involvement of local leadership in the programme were identified as some of the operational constraints in the effective implementation of the ICDS scheme. It was observed that women and community leaders had low level of awareness regarding ICDS programme (Sharma and Sushma, 1986).

In a community only 4 percent respondents could link the scheme with child welfare and only 9 per cent respondents knew that women in the age-group 15—44 years were also among the beneficiary group. They also had limited knowledge about ICDS functionaries and their job responsibilities. However, AWWs and Helpers were better known than CDPOs. Further, the level of knowledge was comparatively higher in rural area than in an urban area (Paranjpe, 1984).

Other researchers (Ramdev, 1982, Sharma, 1986) found that people were aware of the scheme and had fairly adequate information regarding ICDS functionaries and various categories of beneficiaries but had low knowledge about the activities of other voluntary organisations. Variables like age, caste, type of family and literacy level had a significant effect on the knowledge of respondents about ICDS. It was reported that the community perceived non-formal pre-school education as learning of counts though AWW considered pre-school education as a better way to acquire good habits and moral values.

It was found that ANMs and LHVs had not understood the purpose of pre-school education (Rajesh, 1984).

The findings of the limited research studies indicate that participation of the community is only marginal or low in most of ICDS blocks and needs special efforts on behalf of ICDS functionaries to elicit participation to make ICDS programme a success. The data available from the research studies are not given in a systematic manner and are also inadequate.

It is significant to note that until 1965, the performance of the Mahila Mandals was evaluated periodically by the annual conferences of development commissioners of the states.

A brief account of these is given below as indicative of the thinking from time to time. The Development Commissioners' Conference held at Simla in 1955 recommended that since the area of the block was too wide to implement the programmes in all villages with equal intensity, three types of programmes of social education for women should be implemented in each block: (a) a full programme, (b) a large programme, and (c) a small programme. While the full programme should be implemented in at least one village which would serve as a model to other villages, the large and small programmes should be executed in every headquarters village of the Gramsevak and in the remaining villages, respectively.

Another conference held at Nainital in 1956 decided that women's programme should be comprehensive enough to include social welfare and home economics and, keeping in view the availability of limited staff, work should be confined to three to five villages at a time and then gradually extended to other villages in NES blocks.

In the community development blocks, however, the coverage might be increased to ten villages at a time. The

Conference held at Mussoorie in 1957 recommended three types of minimum programmes for women, viz., a universal programme, a secondary programme and a primary programme which were to be implemented in blocks keeping in view the availability of staff and stage of development.

In addition, the need to encourage involvement of scheduled castes and backward castes and classes was also emphasised. Again after one year, a conference held at Mount Abu in 1958 emphasised on the necessity of providing supervision at the state and district levels and decided that the block development officer should be given suitable training in the development of women's programmes.

It also recommended the utilisation of funds under the schemes of the Khadi Commission and other Boards as well as other development departments. Whereas the conference held at Mysore in 1959 expressed the view that the programmes for women and children should be planned and implemented by the Mahila Mandals and the village Panchayats should help them in carrying out their tasks and responsibilities. The Conference held at Hyderabad in 1961 drew up a Minimum Programme for Women which envisaged the organisation of at least ten Mandals in each block with a Balwadi, an Adult Education Centre and a craft or other unit like poultry and kitchen gardening attached to each one of them.

Their activities should include talks and demonstrations at suitable intervals on balanced diet, family planning, training in domestic chores, use of spare time to improve the economic conditions of the family, social education, knowledge of agriculture and animal husbandry, celebration of national days and local festivals, baby shows, study tours, etc. The Conference held at New Delhi in 1962 recognised the need for establishing about 110 Mandals per block. These should be promoted with the help of trained local women such as *Gram Lakshmis* and *Gram Kakis*. The activities should include recreational and cultural programmes, occupational interest, adult literacy, citizenship education, mothers' education including family planning, maternity and child welfare. At the another Conference held at New Delhi in 1963, it was decided that ultimately there should be one Mandal each village that priority should be given to the economic programmes like, horticulture, pisciculture, piggery, poultry, bee-keeping, food processing and preservation, sericulture, kitchen gardening and tailoring.

The Conference of 1964 held at New Delhi recommended that effective use of Mandals should be made in the promotion of production programmes, especially in the activities of mid-day meals in schools, development and management of schools and community gardens, poultry and fishery units. The Srinagar Conference of 1965 decided to eventually establish at least one Mahila Mandal in every village with a population of 500 or more. It decided on giving encouragement to economic projects which could sustain group-interest. A number of measures were considered to strengthen to staff at different levels for implementing various women's programmes. It was felt that the Mandals should be given definite programmes for implementation by the panchayati raj bodies and be provided with the necessary financial resources and technical and administrative supervision.

The Balwantray Mehta Committee (1957), which examined the working of community projects and national extension service had suggested that (i) care of the cow, the kitchen garden and poultry should receive primacy of attention of women workers in the villages, (ii) training in elementary use of thread and needs should be given so that women can mend clothes for the family, (iii) in villages surrounding large towns and cities, cookery classes should be started. Another Committee on Community Development and Panchayati Raj (1976) recommended the promotion and strengthening of these organisations and association of weaker sections in their management. It wanted the Mahila Mandals to give priority to such programmes which would improve their economic conditions.

In 1978, a Working Group constituted for reviewing the objectives and functioning of Mahila Mandals has recommended a new programme in keeping with the new development strategy and objectives of the Sixth Plan. The objective of the programme, the Group observed, "is to draw rural women into the mainstream of development and to enable them to function as instruments of social change by providing them with programmes in which they will have a stake or a sustained interest such as improving their income or productivity and employability or employment."

Calling for a flexible approach in regard to the type of women's organisations in order to meet the needs of different sections of the society, it recommended: (i) the establishment of one Mahila Mandal for every unit of 500 people; (ii) making a block grant of Rs. 1,500 and Rs. 7,500 to each Mahila Mandal for administrative and economic development purposes, respectively, (the latter has to be sanctioned depending on the quality and size of the project planned by the Mandal), (iii) the training of village-level organiser to promote and help the Mandals; (iv) the posting of five field level workers per block and, one officer each at the block, district and state levels; (v) giving representation to Mandals in the panchayats; and (vi) the formation of federations of Mahila Mandals at the block and district levels.

Remarkably, Asoka Mehta Committee on Panchayati Raj Institutions (1978) recommended that the programme for women "should recognise and strengthen their constructive, decision-making and managerial roles so as to enable them to have full access to development resources and services." Emphasising on the importance of the motivational and promotional role of panchayati raj bodies in the women's programme, the Committee recommended for a committee with all women members of the proposed Mandal panchayat represented in it so that decision on priorities and choices in welfare and development programmes meant for them were made by themselves.

The Mahila Mandals are observed to operate with greater flexibility and base their activities on felt needs. Mandals often function more effectively than the Government managed agencies in the areas such as motivation, problem identification and analysis, project formulation, innovation methods of services delivery and involvement of the community due to their spirit. Gandhi (1984) was of the view that an ICDS block, Mahila Mandals and Youth Clubs were actively involved in implementing ICDS programme. They were helping AWWs regularly in all the activities. Even the Programme Evaluation Organisation (PEO) stated that the activities of the Mahila Mandals were moderately successful. Commenting on their performance in the state of Punjab, it stated that the slow progress of these organisations was mainly due to conservatism among women and non-availability of guidance from the concerned extension officers. In Madhya Pradesh, on the other hand, it found that the initial enthusiasm withered away with the passage of time. In its Fourth Report (1957), the PEO concluded that only 8 percent of the villages were covered in most of the community development projects.

Further the Committee on Plan Projects (COPP) found that the activities of the Mandals were largely confined to semiurban villages and even then, very little was done for the women and children belonging to the poorer sections. In its Sixth Report (1959), the PEO reported that the block staff for social education was inadequate and the work was not equally shared by the male and female Social Education Organisers (SEO). It also observed that frequent transfers hampered their effectiveness.

The United Nations Community Development Evaluation Mission in India (1959) found that emphasis in the work of most of the Mandals was on tailoring which was useful only for domestic purpose and not as an income generating activity. It further observed that women, in general, did not want to be categorised as tailors because of the fact that this occupation was considered to be of a low status.

The Seventh Report (1959-60) of the PEO found that the average number of Mandals per block was only eleven. Most of these Mandals had undertaken activities such as propagation of literacy, economic and cultural programmes.

The involvement of Mandals in Applied Nutrition Programme was reviewed by the PEO (1965). It found that while in Orissa and Tamil Nadu the Mandals has done a good job in Supplementary Feeding Programme, the level of their performance in the other two states was below the expectations. In Uttar Pradesh, a number of feeding centres had to be closed as the Mandals were not able to maintain them.

T.K. Oommen (1969) in his study found that out of 59 Mandals, only 25 were functioning. There was a wide gap between their objectives and the actual performance. A majority of the members were found to be middle-caste groups. The activities were generally related to cultural programmes such as *kirtans* and *Bhajans* and occasionally the members held discussions on village sanitation, kitchen gardening or family planning programmes. Some of the difficulties identified were paucity of funds and lack of freedom for women to participate in the activities of the Mandals. Desai and Gaikwad (1971) conducted an evaluative study on Applied Nutrition Programme and found that the participation of the Mandals in programmes other than tailoring and cultural activities was not effective. It was further observed that the tendency among the block officials was to view their responsibility only in terms of establishing the Mandals and providing there with token material and financial assistance without ensuring their meaningful involvement in the programmes.

The Evaluation Committee on Applied Nutrition Programme in Maharashtra (1971) reported that in such places where the Mandals were engaged in the feeding programme, their performance was good. On the contrary, in areas where these organisations were not active, the programme could not achieve success. Another evaluative study conducted by Muthayya and others (1977) at the NIRD concluded that the involvement of the Mandals in ANP was rather marginal. Their participation in the implementation was discretionary rather than obligatory. The potential of the Mandals had not been utilised fully in the management and supervision of the programme. A study by Jain and Reddy (1979) is perhaps the pioneer work on Mahila Mandals which concludes that the contribution of these organisations have made to improving the socio-economic conditions of women on the one hand, and in the overall task of rural development on the other. This is evident from the fact that the activities were invariably oriented towards social welfare programmes. Notwithstanding the shortcomings, the Mandals have played an important role in making the rural women to come out of their homes and interact with the forces of modernization in terms of participation in community affairs besides elevating their own social status.

These have also provided in them a measure of social confidence while dealing with officials and non-officials working at the block and the village levels. The rise in the status of women is evident from the fact that their association with the Mandals has provided them with a measure of respect in the village polity.

Further, he suggests that the entire effort in respect of developing Mahila Mandals has to be viewed from the perspective of human resource development. Whatever investment is made in the promotion on these organisations will ultimately prove to be sound investment in human capital.

Remarkably, another study by Jain (1982) attempts to highlight the pattern of activities of the Bharatiya Grameen Mahila Sangh (BGMS). The study concludes that the BGMS has confined its activities to achieve the objectives through state level branches and other organisations functioning at village level.

Most of the activities are intimately concerned with the development of poor rural women. It's state-level branches have also been assisting the Government machinery in the implementation of some of the programmes mean for the welfare of women and children.

It is pertinent to note that Preeta (1985) was of the view that Mahila Mandals are delivery instruments for services to women and children and these services are broadly determined by central sponsors. They are not set up in such a way as to achieve the goal to integrate rural women in community life and decision-making. Objectives need to be minimised to facilitate the efficient functioning of such institutions. It was also observed that the ICDS faces a lack of cooperation and support from the people. There is no substantial participation at the village level.

Anganwadis are often situated in such locations that one or other section of the village community will not be able to participate. Such communal feelings which seriously affect the implementation of a programme can only be removed if the cooperation of the village leader is obtained.

There is need to have constant feedback from the Mahila Mandals and women groups to strengthen the ICDS services. In order to revitalise the services of ICDS, a study of contribution and involvement of Mahila Mandals/ women groups in the scheme would inevitable.

Remarkably, Nimbkar (1986) has suggested that the Grameen Mahila Mandal could extend its interest and integrate its programme with activities of other village institutions like the local schools by organising school lunch programmes with the local day-nurseries or creche by organising child-care programmes, with the local Balwadi by helping to prepare necessary simple equipment, with local sanitation drives by helping to organise soak-pits, sanitary latrines, etc.

Even Vasu (1990) is of the view the Mahilasamagams in Kerala numbering over 10,000 are often cited as one of the best examples of community participation in social development. They are unique from the point of view of their areas of operation, strength, commitment to social cause and benefits generated for rural women. However, research conducted on this area is too meagre to come to any conclusion. The emphasis has been mostly on social and cultural activities and very little economic orientation has so far been given. Although some of the studies covered here were not directly carried out in respect of Mahila Mandals, they, nevertheless, indicate the extent to which these organisations are involved in different programmes.

REFERENCES

Desai, M.G. and Gaikwad, V.R. (1971) : *ANP : An Evaluation Study,* Centre for Management in Agri., IIM, Ahmedabad, pp. 135 and 189.

Dev Ram, Lal Bindiya (1982) : *Monitoring and Evaluation of Community Participation in an ICDS Project,* Unpublished Report, NIPCCD, New Delhi.

Gandhi, T.B. (1984) : *Community Participation in the Urban ICDS Project Vizag, Andhra Pradesh,* Deptt. of Paediatrics, Andhra Med. College, Visakhapatnam, A.P.

Govt. Of India (1955) : *Summary Record of Fourth Development Commissioners' Conference on Community Projects at Simla* (9-12 May, 1955), Community Projects Administration, August, 1955.

Govt. of India (1956) : *Summary Record of Fifth Development Commissioners' Conference held at Nainital,* (5-7th May 1956), p. 58.

Govt. of India (1978) : *Report of the Committee on Panchayati Raj Institutions* (Chairman : Asoka Mehta), Deptt. of Rural Development, Min. of Agri. and Irri., August, pp. 141-142.

Govt. of India (1978) : *Report of the Working Group on Development of Village-level Organisations of Rural Women,* Deptt. of Rural Development, Min. of Agri. and Irri., June, pp. 4-21.

Govt. of India (1982) : *Integrated Child Development Services Scheme (Revised),* Ministry of Social Welfare, New Delhi, p. 2-3.

Govt. of Maharashtra (1971): *Report of the Evaluation Committee on ANP,* Deptt. of Rural Development, pp. 18-20.

Jain, S.P. (1979) : *Role of Women in Rural Development - A Study of Mahila Mandals,* NIRD, Hyderabad, p. 4.

Jain, S.P. (1982) : *Bhartiya Grameen Mahila Sangh - A Case Study,* NIRD, Hyderabad.

Kumar Rajesh, Prakash, V. and Lal Sunder (1984) : *A Study of Community's Reaction to the Scheme of ICDS and its Package of Services,* Unpublished, Deptt. of Prevention and Social Medicine, Medical College, Rohtak, Haryana.

Murthy, L.S.N. and Mathur, S. (1988) : *Project Management - A Study of ICDS Projects,* NIPCCD, New Delhi, p. 1.

Muthayya, B.C. and et. al. (1978) : *Evaluation of ANP,* Interim Report presented at National Seminar on ANP Held at NIRD, Hyderabad, August 28-31, p. 35.

Nimbkar, K.B. (1986) : *Development Work among Rural Women - A Guide Book,* Indian Adult Ed. Association, New Delhi, pp. 31-32.

Oomen, T.K. (1969) : 'Mahila Mandals in Rural Delhi,' *Social Welfare,* Vol. No. 16(5), August, pp. 11-12.

Paranjpe, Rajni K. and Bhagwat, Rewati (1984) : *A Study of Perception and Participation of the Community in ICDS in Maharashtra,* Unpublished, Mimeograph, College of Social Work, Bombay.

Preeta, L. (1985), 'Rural Development : Its impact on Women, *Social Action,* Vol. 35(1), Jan.-March, pp. 81-90.

Programme Evaluation Organisation (1958): *Evaluation Report on the Working of Community Projects and NES Blocks,* Govt. of India, Planning Commission, pp.55, 195, 221.

Sharma, Sushma and Chand Gayatri (1986) : *Perception and Participation of the Community in ICDS,* unpublished, Deptt., of Foods and Nutrition, Lady Irwin College, New Delhi.

Vasu, E. (1990): 'Mahilasamajam Movement in Kerala,' *Social Welfare,* Vol. XXVII, No. 7, Oct. pp. 20-33.

6

Role of Women's Groups

> "We work day after day, not to finish things; but to make the future better..... because we will spend the rest of our lives there."
>
> —*Charles F. Kattering*

In fact, group dynamics of potential tool for human resource development. In case of women role of group becomes more vital.

In the present chapter we have tried to elucidate the role of groups for women resource development. Various groups working on this theme are discussed herein.

Women's Groups are an important part of the strategy for women's involvement in several development and welfare programmes, such as, Indira Mahila Yojana, Rashtriya Mahila Kosh, World Bank assisted ICDS Programme IFAD, Family Welfare Programme. Adult Education, DWACRA and NABARD. These groups, formed at the village level constitute an easily accessible forum for women to discuss problems relating to their daily life, their status and role within the family and society, and their self-image as women. These Women's groups carry the message of the programmes to the community and create awareness on the issues of specific concern to women and mobilise the support of the community functionaries to facilitate the implementation of the programmes.

Mahila Sanghas

Mahila Sanghas are women's groups formed under the programme of Mahila Samakhya which aims at achieving equality through education. These Sanghas are a forum for discussion of women's problems particularly, those related to their self-image as women. They set out their own agenda for education and collective action. So far over 4,826 Sanghas have been formed.

World Bank Assisted ICDS

Under the World Bank assisted ICDS I and II Projects income generation activities are carried out through active Mahila Mandals/Women's groups. These groups are given financial assistance for providing training and skill upgradation and taking up income generation activities.

Mahila Swasthya Sanghs

These women's groups are trained to undertake health education and communication activities in the community. The thrust areas are raising of age at marriage, safe motherhood, child survival, immunisation, ORT and spacing and permanent methods of family planning.

DWACRA

The Development of Women and Children in Rural Areas, Programme aims at improving women's access to the services like health, education, nutrition, water and sanitation. Under the programme poor rural women are organised into women's groups and provided training assistance under TRYSEM programme and subsidy for taking up group economic activities for income generation. At least 1.85 lakh groups have been formed till now.

Indira Mahila Yojana

As we all know, people's participation is an essential ingredient that makes a development programme palatable. Many a ambitious schemes have met its Waterloo because it failed to stir up the interest of the intended beneficiaries. It is, therefore necessary that participants of any scheme, whether they are part of the delivery system or the actual recipients of the package at the grassroots, get a sense of involvement in scheme as a whole.

A feeling that they are participating in the betterment of their own future will lend a purpose to the planning, help develop their capabilities and give them a sense of responsibility. The last three decades have seen several development schemes targeting the women population of the country. The aim has been to achieve betterment of women particularly the rural and tribal women. To a large extent the schemes have delivered results. Some of them are the ICDS, WDP and DWACRA. They have also been extended benefits under JRY, TRYSEM, Literacy Missions etc. These have expanded quantitatively over the years and the delivery system of some of these programmes have shown qualitative results too. While some programmes have been implemented entirely by Government machinery, there are schemes which are NGO oriented.

Remarkably, the economic liberalisation has brought in its wake the concept of 'single window' clearance — that is setting up of a central focal point where a person can get all necessary Govt. approvals and need not run from pillar to post. If such an idea results in making life less cumbersome and easy for its beneficiaries why cannot this concept be imported into the social development field too? There should be a focal point where women should be able to reach for all the benefits that they can get. It is from this thinking process that the idea of convergence of services in form of IMY was born.

The Indira Mahila Yojana is nothing but bringing together various health, nutrition development and other welfare programmes for women under a single umbrella. Thus this per se is not a new scheme but a amalgam of the existing schemes. Thus the philosophy behind IMY makes the earlier concepts of social development programmes stand on its head! Here the prioritisation of the programmes will be done by the beneficiaries who will plan at the block level. The block level plan (normally the size of ICDS block) will find its place in district plan which in turn will merge with the State-level Plan.

Thus the women beneficiaries turn into thinkers, anlaysers and planners. Be it health, nutritious, sanitation, drinking water or creating income -generation activity they will be in a position to decide and articulate their needs. There is, however, the realisation that IMY, being a non-conventional programme aimed at being the convergence point of several schemes, in itself has no trained personnel to help women articulate their needs.

There are no designated functionaries except community participants in position. No built-in training schemes. Like the elected women members of Panchayat, women members of IMY blocks will be thrown into the ring and will have to fend for themselves unaided and unguided.

Training Programmes Under IMY

Training is important in any development programmes. This is particularly true of IMY as it aims to bring about awareness, attitudinal changes, gender sensitisation, building up of leadership quality and help develop decision-making capacity in women. IMY, being a new and unique concept with the aim of achieving effective convergence of all women related development schemes of Centre and State, calls for a high degree of consideration and co-operation among various government departments implementing the scheme, NGOs and Women's group.

It follows that such a comprehensive scheme will have a large target group that would require to be trained. There would be, in addition to training needs of women's groups, need to orient officials and non-officials connected with IMY.

Focus of Training

(i) IMY ideology

(ii) Awareness generation

(iii) Group dynamics

(iv) Accounts & procedures of IMK

(v) Specialised training for economic activity.

(vi) Monitoring & EDP training.

Target Group for Training

As per the present scheme of IMY, there will be a Indira Mahila Block Samiti (IMBS) under which a number of Indira Mahila Kendras (IMK) will function. Ideally each ICDS block will have one IMBS and one IMK will function in each village (or for each anganwadi target group of 1000 population). Each IMK will have about 25-30 members. One member of each IMK will be identified as its leader called the President or the animator. There will be about 100 IMK in each Block depending on the number of anganwadi, in a ICDs Block. The proposal is to introduce IMY in 200 blocks during 1996-97 including in 30 blocks in U.P.

	U.P.	All India
No. of IMBS	30	200
No. of IMK	3000*	20,000
No. of animators	3,000	20,000
No. of officials	90	600
Total no. of members	75,000*	5,00,000

* Estimated on the basis that there are 100 anganwadi centres in each block.

Since there is a large universe to be trained, the number to be trained from each block/IMK can be varied and the target for 1996-97 fixed.

Types of Training Modules (for Training/Orienting Animators and Members)

Following are some of the options available for being adopted:

Sandwich Pattern

The animators of the IMBS and IMK will be oriented and trained for 6 days at the first instance. This will be the Phase I or the institutional training and the inputs will comprises of:

(a) general orientation in LMY concepts.

(b) orientation to programmes and policies of the Government.

(c) group formation methodologies identification of scheme.

(d) maintenance of record and registers.

(e) identification of income generation activities etc.

Phase II will mainly concentrate on the field activity. The animators will then be sent back to the field to carry out these activities. A NGO will be guiding the animators in their activity. As per the existing scheme each IMK will have a corpus of Rs. 5000/-. Membership fee at the admission stage is Rs 5/- and for subsequent months Re 1/-. The IMK and the animator can utilise this fund to meet the orientation needs of other members and for forming the group.

After six months the animators will again be called for the Phase-III of the course. The animators will undergo skill-training in economic development activities such as organising marketing, liaisoning with banks and officials and promoting other activities or IMK. This will act as refresher course to clarify various issues. The duration of the course could be between 3 days to 6 days depending upon the syllabus evolved.

The programme would therefore involve 12 days training. Cost per person will be, at the rate of Rs. 40/- per person, Rs. 480/-. The institutional training could be assigned to an NGO having the infrastructural facilities to conduct the programme for at least 30-50 persons at a time. The training infrastructure, available with the State Government such as NIPCCD (RC), ITIs, SIRDs, can also be used. It should however be ensured that some organisation monitors the entire sandwich course.

IFAD (International Fund for Agriculture Development) Model

This is a more complex model and envisages a training programme in greater detail. Presently this is being tried out in five-districts of Tamilnadu. Since its object is mainly social and economic upliftment of women and enhancing the status of the community, the animators undergo a detailed training of 40 days comprising of 32 days training module and 8 days refreshers module.

The expenses per person per day are Rs. 60/-. Thus training a single animator would cost Rs. 2400/-.

While adopting IFAD model it may not be necessary to having as many as eleven modules for the animators. Instead there can be only four modules totalling 12-14 days, The cost per animator can thus be kept at about Rs. 700/-.

Like the sandwich pattern, the training in IFAD model will also have to be entrusted to NGO-run institutions. Only difference is the trainers of NGO will have to go to the project area or the Block area and conduct the programme. For this purpose it may be necessary to train the trainers of NGO, identified for the purpose of the scheme, at a central organisation such as NIPCCD (RC) SIRD etc. The advantage of this method is that the animators, who are in effect only volunteers can attend the programme without their family life being disrupted. Secondly, the trainers themselves, being at block level, will be able to relate to the field situations. This can be effective method of monitoring the programme by getting feedback from the trainers.

The NGO will also feel involved in the Block development and can therefore act as facilitators in co-ordinating the EDP programmes with lead banks/WDCs etc.

Mobile in Service Training

The concept of mobile in-service training was tried out by a N.G.O. Crime Prevention Trust, Ahmedabad in collaboration with USAID in Panchmahal District, Gujarat. This concept was extended to ICDS projects in Gujarat and Maharashtra with the assistance of UNICEF. A team of trained instructors were deployed to organise training programmes at civil level in a ICDS block. Supervisors were first trained at block level before going to circle level where supervisor assists MIST trainers.

The duration of the training programme varied between 3-5 days to 5-7 days according to the level of official undergoing training. Trainee batch usually comprised of 40-50 persons. The mobile unit naturally depended on audio-visual method. Overall cost for mounting such a scheme is likely to be high as the scheme has to provide for vehicles audio-visual equipments for its repairs and for the training software besides adequate staff like trainees, driver, technical staff etc.

Remarkably, the main advantages are: (i) flexible training time which can be helpful in rural and tribal areas where women work during the day; (ii) use of audio-visual method which can help larger coverage of not only animators but also the beneficiaries, (mobile units) accessibility to remote areas; (iii) it will help save women from leaving their homes; (iv) it will promote co-operation and build up relationship between trainees to ensure sharing of experience. Another immediate gain will be use of the mobile infrastructure for publicising the scheme itself for under the scheme there is a provision for a one time grant of which the scheme provides for Rs. 10,000 to each NGO.

Thus over a period of time due to its coverage ability the cost may even out. In order to introduce MIST in IMY it will be necessary to identify a State training centre which can conduct block level training for NGOs and the trainers of NGOs can then go to circles/IMK centres. The training cost will mainly comprise of vehicle maintenance, staff salary and their TA/DA.

Proposed Orientation Scheme Under Panchayati Raj

Two training models are under consideration for

orienting women members of Panchayati Raj. The first model is to organise a seven day orientation programme at block/district level. Since the animators of IMY will be, in terms of qualification and experience, similar to Panchayat Members, a similar programme can be organised at block level by the state training centres. The cost of training per person per day will be about Rs. 40%. The only disadvantage is that due to vastness of number to be oriented it may take very long for few institutions to achieve 100% coverage.

In model II a state level training centre will first train trainers of Anganwadi Workers Training Centre (AWTCs). These trainers will in turn organise 7-15 days training programme at AWTCs for the panchayat raj representatives. Similar approach can be adopted for training the animators of IMY. These animators can then impart training to members of IMY. As and when refresher courses are orgnaised, feedback can be obtained.

Distance Education

The training scheme for IMY envisages provision of adequate number of audio equipments at block level. These equipments will be maintained by district officials or NGOs and can be utilised for holding group services at IMK/IMBS levels. Lessons can be prepared and cassettes sent to these blocks at frequent intervals by the State training centres. This will be kin to UGC educational programme. The scheme will, however require lot of commitment on the part of district officials/NGOs. It will also require provision for giving cassette players (one big and one portable) besides regular supply of educational cassettes.

Training Pattern Under EDP Pilot Schemes Thro Lead Banks

While planning training schemes under IMY, it would

be useful to keep in mind the training scheme presently organised by lead banks in sect districts. These are aimed at providing the beneficiaries with Economic Development activity. The banks have evolved training packages and impart the training themselves. For this purpose officials involved in implementing the pilot scheme are trained by organising 2-3 days sessions. They in turn; with the help of NGOs, undertake training programmes for the beneficiaries. In order to cover the economic development component the IMY training programmes, whatever model is adopted, can include the lead bank capsule as one of the component.

Importance of training for effective implementation of IMY is reflected in the IMY manual but not the magnitude of the task of training. Only when we get down to the nitty-gritty of organising training programmes do we realise that there is no single universally applicable strategy that can work. The social and cultural diversity and the difference in the levels of social consciousness and economic backwardness require diversity in approach. The success or failure of the programme would largely depend on the effectiveness of the NGOs. But not all NGOs are of the same calibre. Setting up of State-run training centres may constitute a heavy financial burden or the exchequer. For e.g., the cost of training at the elected women members of Panchayat is estimated at Rs. 73 crores. The number of members under the IMY being larger, the cost will be many folds.

All these factors will have to be kept in view by the respective State-level planners while opting for the training model suitable for their State. Ultimately proof of the pudding is the eating and training is only a means to an end, the end being upliftment of backward and poor women of this country

Sandwich Pattern

Advantages	Disadvantages
1. Training related to work and actual situation	1. Difficulties in coordination of three phases for trainees
2. Cost effective	2. Lack of proper monitoring and supervisio
3. Better Coordination between field officials and AWTCs	3. Possibility of dropout in 3rd phase.
4. Opportunities for skill development	4. Entirely dependent on quality of NGO service.

Mobile Inservice Training (MIST)

1. Field based, need based	1. Trainers may not be willing to move from place to place.
2. Can achieve greater coverage of target beneficiaries	2. No proper training infrastructure set up
3. Convenient for trainees — need not leave the family to get trained	3. Cost of vehicle maintenance and equipments may be higher.
4. Trainers can go to remote places	
5. Flexible training hours	
6. Audio-visual presentation by trainers can help mobilise local support.	

Panchayat Model (Institutional Training)

1. Availability of good infra-structure facilities	1. Motivating women to attend training in a institutional set up may not be easy task
2. Competent trained trainers	2. Ignorance, fear of loss or wages, lack of support from other members of family and the inability to get away may come in the way of women members attending the training.
	3. The massive training infrastructure may be difficult to sustain in terms of funds, motivation etc.

Distance Education

	Advantages		*Disadvantages*
1.	Economical as it involves centralised preparation of training/awareness generation material	1.	Lack of field related activities
2.	Adaptible to local situation, language etc.	2.	Less effective for imparting skill training.
3.	Flexible hours possible	3.	No check on actual importing of training

MAHILA SAMRIDDHI YOJANA

The Government has started a scheme called Mahila Samriddhi Yojana (MSY) which was launched on 2nd October, 1993. The scheme aims to promote self-reliance and a measure of economic independence among rural women. Government has taken this important step in its effort to change inequalities in social construction of gender particularly in rural areas. MSY is encouraging thrift among rural women so that they can start their savings and be assured of security in times of need. This will also give experience and confidence to women to operate their accounts independently and have control over household resources.

Women's Own Account

Under the MSY, every rural woman aged 18 and above is being encouraged to have any MSY account of her own in the local post office in which she can deposit the amount of money she can save. The response to this scheme has been encouraging throughout the length and breadth of the country.

Operation of the Mahila Samriddhi Yojana

The operation of this scheme has been made very simple. Each adult rural woman can deposit in her MSY account upto Rs. 300 in a year. She can open the MSY account with just Rs. 4 and its multiples. While opening the MSY account, the woman can certify her own name, age and address. Noone else is required to provide such a certificate. She can open MSY account in Post Office having jurisdiction over the village in which she lives. The account gets opend on the day of first deposit and a receipt is issued. A Pass Book shall also be issued within a week indicating the date and amount of deposit. Facilities for nomination are also provided to the account holders.

How MSY Benefits Rural Women

For an amount of upto Rs. 300 kept in the Post Office for a lock-in-period of one year, the government will give an incentive of 25 per cent. That means the MSY account holder will get Rs. 375 (Rs. 300 deposit + Rs. 75 incentive) on a deposit of Rs. 300 after the year. The government will give a maximum contribution of Rs. 75 in a year corresponding to a deposit of Rs. 300. If the amount deposited is less, the incentive will be proportionately less.

If the need arises, MSY account holder can withdraw money twice in a year. Even then she is entitled to an incentive at the rate of 12 per cent per annum on the withdrawn amount if it has remained in the account, for more than 30 days. Besides MSY account, rural women can also open any other account under other schemes.

Whom to Contact For More Information

1. Post Master of the post office which has jurisdiction over your village.
2. Supervisor/Anganwadi Worker for your village
3. Gram Sevika of your village.

Open Your MSY Account Today

"The Mahila Samriddhi Yojana is receiving a very enthusiastic response from rural women. I am overwhelmed by this response.

The monetary saving is only a part of the intended benefit. The real gain is the sense of financial self-reliance that woman gets when she acquires her won independent savings account.

I am convinced that this small step, however, unspectacular, carries within it a whole world of change in the outlook, and thereby in the status of one half of Indian population".

P.V. Narasimha Rao

Prime Minister

"The Scheme aims at promoting and encouraging rural women to save by providing direct cash incentives to supplement their individual savings. Such gender specific interventions are necessary to ensure that the benefit directly flows to beneficiaries".

Arjun Singh

Minister of Human Resource Development

"This scheme would not only provide a sense of security to our rural women but also help in raising their status and triggering attitudinal changes in society towards them.

Basavarajeswari

Minister of State

Women and Child Development

PART I
SECTION 1
MINISTRY OF HUMAN RESOURCE DEVELOPMENT
(Department of Women and Child Development)

NOTIFICATION
NEW DELHI, THE 29TH SEPTEMBER, 1993
THE MAHILA SAMRIDDHI YOJANA

No. 19-31/93-CW.—The Government of India hereby notifies the following Scheme with effect from October 1, 1993 relating to Mahila Samriddhi Yojana until further orders:

1. Short Title and Extent

(a) This Scheme may be called Mahila Samriddhi Yojana, 1993.

(b) It covers all women who are of 18 or more years of age and are residents of rural area.

2. Definitions

(a) "Account" means an account to which this Scheme applies,

(b) "Rural Area" means areas other than urban areas as defined by the 1991 Census of India.

(c) "Depositor" means a rural adult women of 18 years or more of age residing in a village served by a Post Office,

(d) "Deposit" means amount deposited by a depositor at a time in her account, but does not include the amount of incentive credited to the account,

(e) "Post Office" means a post office which has delivery jurisdiction where the depositor's village is located,

(f) "Form A-D" means form A to D appended to the Notification,

(g) "Head Postmaster" means an officer-in-charge of Head Post Office and includes a Deputy Postmaster or an Assistant Postmaster to whom the powers of the Head Postmaster have been delegated.

3. Opening of Mahila Samriddhi Yojana Account

A depositor desiring to open an account in a Post Office may make an application to it in Form-A. The depositor at the time of opening of account will give a declaration on the application that she is 18 years or more of age and resident of the village mentioned therein and has got no other Mahila Samriddhi Yojana Account in any other post office.

4. Place of Deposit

The amount will be accepted for deposit only where the account stands.

5. Mode of Deposit

(a) Deposit will be made in cash only,

(b) No account will be opened with a deposit of less than Rupees four.

(c) No subsequent deposit shall be of a sum of less than Rupees four,

(d) The deposits which are not in multiples of Rupees four shall not be accepted,

(e) Maximum amount deposited in an account will not exceed Rupees three hundred at any time,

(f) Every deposit will have a lock-in period of one year unless withdrawn as per the Scheme.

6. Incentive

(a) The incentive will be paid on those deposits which are kept with the Post Office for a period of one year from the date of its deposit,

(b) Incentive at the rate of twenty-five per cent of the deposit may be paid on completion of a lock-in-year with a maximum of Rupees seventy-five on deposits up to Rupees three hundred,

(c) In case of withdrawal of a deposit before a lock-in period/closure of account prematurely, incentive will be payable at the rate of 12 per cent per annum on the deposit remaining with the post office between thirty days and less than one year. No incentive would be paid on deposit remaining with the post office for a fraction part of thirty days :

Provided the incentive due on such withdrawals shall be payable only at the time when any deposit becomes due for payment on maturity.

Provided further their case of premature closure of account, the amount of incentive, if any, due shall become due for payment on the date of the closure of the account.

7. Withdrawals

Not more than two withdrawals will be allowed from an account in a calendar year. The amount of each withdrawal shall be in multiples of Rupees four with a minimum of Rupees twenty. The incentive on the deposits remaining with the post office shall be payable at the rate and in the manner as mentioned in para 6(c).

8. Premature Closure

A depositor shall be entitled to close the account at any timeafter its opening and shall be paid the incentive at the rates and in the manner mentioned in para 6(c). In case where the depositor has closed the account, she will not be permitted to open another account in that calendar year.

9. Identification of the Depositor

Identification of a depositor at the time of closure shall ordinarily be made by verification of her signature appearing on the record in the Post Office and in cases where identification cannot be done as aforesaid, it may be done in such other manner as may be notified by the Director General, Department of Posts.

10. Passbook

(a) On opening of an account, the depositor shall be given a pass book, bearing the number of her account, her name, her address, and entry of her first deposit duly signed by an authorised official of the Post Office.

(b) It shall be the responsibility of the depositor to keep the passbook in safe custody.

(c) If the passbook is lost, stolen, destroyed or spoilt while in custody of the depositor, she shall be issued a duplicate passbook on her paying a fee of Rs. 5.00 and on completion of such inquiries as the Post Office may consider necessary and no such fee shall be charged if the Head Postmaster is satisfied that the circumstances in which the passbook was lost, stolen, destroyed or spoiled were beyond the control of the depositor,

(d) No deposit or withdrawal will be made without production of passbook,

(e) When the passbook is returned duly completed, the depositor shall bring the errors or omission therein, if any, to the notice of the Post Office forthwith and in the event of the depositors' failure to do so, the Post Office shall not be responsible for any loss arising from such errors or omission.

11. Transfer of an Account

No transfer of account will be permissible from one Post Office to another under any circumstances.

12. Closure of Account

Closure of account at an Extra Department Branch Post Office or Extra Department Sub-Office shall be allowed only after obtaining the sanction of Accounts Office/Head Office, Departmental Sub-Post Office will be authorised to close the account independently.

13. Nomination and Repayment

(a) A depositor may nominate in Form 'D' or as near thereto as possible one or more persons to receive the amount standing to her credit in the event of her death before the account has become payable, or having become payable has not been paid;

(b) A nomination made by a depositor may be cancelled or varied by a nomination in Form "C" or as near thereto as possible by giving notice in writing to the Post Office in which the account stands;

(c) Every nomination and every cancellation or variation thereof shall be registered in the Head Post Office and shall be effective from the date of such registration the particular of which shall be entered in the passbook;

(d) If any nominee is a minor, the depositor may appoint any person to receive the amount due under the account in the event of the death of the depositor during the minority of the nominee;

(e) Notwithstanding the provisions contained above :

(i) If a depositor of an account in respect of which a nomination is in force dies, the nominee, or nominees may make an application in Form "D" or as near thereto as possible, to the accounts office together with proof of death of the depositor and on receipt of such application all amounts standing to the credit of the depositor after making adjustment, if any, in respect of incentive shall be repaid by the post Office itself to the nominee or nominees;

Provided that if any nominee is dead, the surviving nominee or nominees shall, in addition to the proof of death of depositor, also furnish proof of the deceased nominee,

(ii) Whether there is no nomination in force at the time of the death of the depositor, the amount standing to the credit of the deceased after making adjustment, if any, shall be repaid by the Post Office only to the legal heirs of the deceased on receipt of application in Form "D" in this behalf from them;

Provided that the balance in the account may be paid to the legal heirs on production of (i) a letter of indemnity, (ii) an affidavit, (iii) a letter of disclaimer on affidavit, and (iv) a certificate of death of subscriber, on stamped papers, in the form in annexures to Form "D".

14. Confirmation of Balance

The depositor shall present her pass book as soon as possible after 30th of June every year to the Post Office where her account stands for confirmation of balance amount at her credit.

15. Recovery of Amount Paid in Excess

The Head Postmaster shall be competent to recover any amount paid in excess in the same manner as arrears of land revenue.

16. Responsibility of the Post Office

The Post Office shall not be (a) responsible to a depositor for any fraudulent withdrawal by a person obtaining possession of the passbook, (b) liable if any fraud takes place due to failure of the depositor to ensure that the amount sought to be withdrawn is entered in the application for withdrawal before the same is presented at or sent duly signed by her to Post Office for withdrawal, and (c) responsible to a depositor, if she or, in case the withdrawal form is presented by messenger, the messenger, fails to ensure that the receipt for the payment is signed by her or the messenger, as the case may be only at the time of actual payment and not at the time of presentation of the application for withdrawal.

17. Power to Relax

Where the Central Government is satisfied that the operation of any of the provision of this Scheme causes undue hardship to a depositor, it may, by order for reasons to be recorded in writing, relax the requirement of that provision in a manner not inconsistent with the provision of the notification.

18. Power to Amend the Scheme

The Central Government shall have the power to amend the Scheme from time to time.

19. Interpretation

If any question arises relating to the interpretation of any relevant provision it shall be referred to the Central Government for a decision.

Meenaxi Anand Chaudhry
Joint Secretary

7

Women Resource Development: Problems of Concepts and Assumptions

Early on in the Second UN Development Decade, it was argued that lack of concern for women's economic participation was reflected in the absence of statistical data on it. The call then was for statisticians to provide disaggregated data because the 'invisibilisation' of women was not only detrimental to women themselves, but was having a negative effect on development itself.

By disaggregation and improving data collection processes and techniques, women's contribution to development could be quantified (and women more efficiently utilised): 'Women who comprise half the population, can and do make enormous contributions to development in all nations.

Without adequate statistical description, their current contributions remain invisible and the barriers to promoting their future contributions to the development process remain hidden' (INSTRAW, 1984, p. 6). Considerable efforts have been made since then to overcome the difficulties in collecting data on women's activities, and an enormous amount of data at national and local levels is now available to researchers and planners. Nonetheless a number of problems still remain: like other 'hard data', much of the information is unreliable, inaccurate and often out of date (Evans, 1990). Definitions can vary between censuses, making comparisons over time difficult. For example, in India a change in the definition of economic activity reduced the female labour force participation rate by an estimated 23 per cent between the censuses of 1961 and 1971.

The lack of standardisation across national boundaries also makes comparative work hazardous. Although there are international conventions on the collection of much macro-level data, different countries still adopt different definitions and ways of measuring economic activity, employment and underemployment, income distribution, and so on.

By the 1990s it is recognised that despite having disaggregated data, women's contribution to national economic well-being is still not being adequately recorded. This is for two main reasons. Because women work in non-market, informal and subsistence sectors, it is still very difficult to record and quantify their participation; it remains largely invisible. But more critically, because the bulk of what women do (i.e. household and family work) is not recognised as productive work it goes unrecorded.

In other words, the way economic activity is conceptualised has a profound affect on what is measured and what is not. Concentration on amassing disaggregated data led to the neglect of a more critical task — uncovering the stereotypes about women (and men), which inform the conceptual categories used in the creation of data. These stereotypes, which come from looking at the world as if all economic actors are male and with archetypal male characteristics, are held by planners, economists and statisticians alike.

Yet the categories themselves have the effect of undercounting and undervaluing the activities and economic contribution of women.

Economic Activity

The production of goods and services —turn on a distinction between productive and unproductive work, but the boundary between there is notoriously vaguely set. This poses particular problems when it comes to measuring the nature and importance of women's economic participation. A great deal of what women do, whether in LDCs or IMEs — processing, preparing and cooking raw food; caring for children and old people; cleaning and washing — is not considered productive. 'But why should preparing and processing food for own-consumption be considered any less productive than growing the food? Why should caring for children be considered less productive than caring for livestock?' (Evans, 1990, p. 9). Why should a man who works in the water board that brings water to the town be considered a productive worker while a woman who carries water from the well to her family is not?

Remarkably, the most The standard answer is, of course, that typical women's work does not involve the market. A less common response implicates widely held preconceptions about the economic activities of men and women and the biological or 'natural' basis of the division of labour between the sexes, particularly as regards work around what can be called human resource production and maintenance (Young, 1987a). If this is thought of as activity deriving from women's natural capacity of child-bearing, then a whole range of tasks can be subsumed under this, made invisible ('my wife doesn't work, she looks after the house') and thus excluded from the category economic.

Stereotypes about women clearly affect the evaluation of their activities. Even within the category of activities considered productive, there are still further problems. Statistics are collected on labour force participation rates, the available pool of workers and their employment status (own account, employer, employee), and levels of employment and unemployment.

But as we saw in the discussion of the informal sector, much of what goes on in developing economies fits poorly into conceptual categories derived from a different economic reality. Recently, further categories have been developed to accommodate more accurately societies where the bulk of the population is not in regular wage work: these include *underemployment*, for which the criterion is either working for abnormally long hours or for disproportionately low wages. However, as yet, categorisations of underemployment are neither consistently, nor widely applied. The economically inactive are all those who cannot clearly be defined as engaging in productive activity or attempting to do so. Unpaid family workers are included if they contribute 'at least a third of normal working hours' to an economic enterprise, but excluded are students, those totally dependent on others, the retired and 'women who are full-time home-makers' (Boulding, 1983, p. 288). There is also no consensus as to the minimum number of hours that an individual has to spend on an economic activity before this gets recognition, and census data in differing countries vary widely.

Magdalena Leon noted in 1984 that 'in six Latin American counties no minimum time is stipulated;... and in seven a period of between one and 18 hours per week is laid down' (Leon, 1984, p. 14). Censuses rarely distinguish between principal and secondary activity: of the 145 censuses carried out between 1955 and 1964 by those UN members which collected occupational information, only 27 asked the respondents about their secondary occupation (Dixon, 1982, p. 543).

If only one activity occupying a fixed amount of time is recorded for each individual, those who carry out multiple activities but spend less time than the defined amount in each (typically a female pattern) will be classified as inactive.

Collecting Data on Women's Activities

Apart from general problems in getting accurate statistical data, what are the major difficulties facing those trying to get data on women? The first major difficulty lies in recording women's economic activities. To begin with both interviewer and respondent are likely to hold preconceptions, which will produce an undercount of women's activities — for example, fetching wood and water is a household task and therefore not 'work' worthy of recording. As was observed wryly by a UN statistician, the woman hauling a 20 litre drum of water to the house is engaged in unproductive (not recordable) activity; her husband laying pipes to bring water to the village is doing both productive work and a recordable activity. Interviewers may expect and therefore elicit stereotypical answers, for example, 'your wife doesn't work, does she?' No she doesn't work, she looks after the family.' Respondents may give the census enumerator the expected answer for a range of reasons including desire to please, perceptions of class difference, and cultural proscriptions. Women themselves may adhere to cultural norms which encourage them to undervalue and underestimate their work: I'm only a housewife. In Sen's terms, their perceived contribution and their own valuation of its worth is low.

Then translating census questions into local languages

always presents difficulties, particularly if the question implies a way of thinking about the organisation of activity which is foreign to the culture itself. For example, in many cultures no separation is made conceptually or linguistically between activities relating to the home and the farm (see Evans, 1990). An easy way to solve this is to omit the activities entirely.

Women's work is more vulnerable to omissions of this kind because interviewers and respondents alike may use a mental mapping which allocates many of women's tasks to housework (i.e. not work) and most of men's to economic activity: consider, for example, the linguistic nicety which allows that women garden while men farm. And even if inter-viewers do try to get data on domestic activities a second set of problems arises: how to distinguish household activities which are 'economic' from the daily processes of living or even leisure. Should making crafts, knitting, going to the market with a few bunches of herbs or growing vegetables in the garden, be regarded as leisure despite the fact that they have an income or income-replacing component?

The second difficulty is how to measure and give a value to activities usually described as domestic? For example, home production. Should it be measured in terms of inputs or outputs; the volume or value of the goods or services produced; the market wage foregone (for further discussion see Goldschmidt-Clermont, 1982).

One strategy would be to include only those activities that correspond or contribute to market-directed activities — e.g. food processing, collecting firewood and water, making tools, utensils and clothing, making crafts. Another would be to define active labour 'in relation to its contribution to the production of goods and services for the satisfaction of human needs. Whether this production is channelled through the market and whether it contributes directly to the accumulation process... should not bias our understanding of what constitutes economic activity' (Beneria, 1982, p. 129). When Lourdes Beneria's recommendation is heeded and home production is acknowledged and added to market work, women's and children's contribution in work time to household welfare is often greater than men's. Using this method on data from the Philippines, King and Evenson (1983) produce some thought-provoking results: husbands contribute most in terms of average market income, but when full income (a combination of payment for market work plus the value of time devoted to home production) is considered, the picture changes dramatically. While men contribute 58 per cent of market income, they only contribute 34 per cent of full income, the remainder being made up by women and children.

King and Evenson note that: '...the importance of non-market production to household welfare and income cannot be overemphasised' (King and Evenson, 1983, p. 51).

Further, a third problem is the fact that men's work pattern is taken as the norm. Census enumerators generally only ask about the primary or main activity a person undertakes; but women's work patterns are more likely to be multiple, part-time and involve moving between economic and non-economic spheres. As this pattern is unlike men's, these activities are often by-passed. This gives rise to a fourth problem: the minimum number of hours that has to be spent on an acitivity per day or per week before it can be officially recognised as economic. Because women frequently carry out various acitivities in parallel (cooking food to be sold later while washing clothes for money; caring for own children while making clothes for sale), it is impossible to keep accurate records (even mental records) of time spent on any one activity.

The easiest way for census takers to solve the problem is to ignore the activities and to categorise the woman's status as 'housewife'. It is thus theoretically possible for a woman who works a 35-hour week but in seven different activities and for only five hours a week in each to be classified as economically inactive. Fifthly and closely connected to this point, are the issues of the reference period and time-scale used when collecting data on economic activity. In most rural areas, production activities vary widely by season, yet census takers come in one season, usually the dry one since travelling is then easier.

In that season little work may be being done as far as cultivation is concerned, except possibly harvesting. People are asked to give details of their economic activities over a relatively brief reference period (one or two weeks is the standard). Recording only dry season low-activity rates, a great deal of crucial activity is excluded from the record. Research indicates that collecting information on women's activities is particularly badly affected if their work at the time of the census is not on-farm but in household/domestic work (confirming the stereotype). Even if the census takers do ask about rainy season activities (when people are often busiest), the problem of respondent recall enters (and how people are prompted). Studies on this show both under-and over -reporting. Both unseasonal time of year and limited reference periods are among the technical explanations for the under-reporting and misrepresentation of women's work in agricultural statistics. Some evidence of urban annual labour patterns would suggest that seasonality of work may also be a feature of urban labour markets but as little systematic work has as yet been done on this, the degree of under-reporting is not yet as issue.

Lastly, as previously touched on, many (especially urban)

informal sector activities may be overlooked in data collection because they are small-scale, highly mobile, seasonal, or culturally disapproved of. Women are not only often disproportionately represented in this sector, but they also will tend to be at the most casualised, least regulated and most insecure end of the informal continuum — thus even harder to capture in aggregate statistics.

Now arise the question—what can be done to rectify the situation? Statisticians have been trying to modify their census categories, adding new ones and so on. Clearly they have to walk the tightrope of simplifying without over-simplification. They have to exclude certain activities if the term 'economic' is to have any meaning. However, to exclude all the work that goes into producing the human resources without which no economic activity would occur seems perverse unless one accepts the premise that what women do in this regard is a natural aspect of their condition of being a woman.

It is in this sense that what is most needed is for the conceptual model that lies behind the census categories to be brought out into the open, contested and changed. Once it is agreed that producing human resources is a productive economic activity, then ways will be found to categorise it for inclusion in censuses, and a means to collect data systematically will be devised. We have ourselves suggested that all the tasks associated with the rearing, care and socialisation of children should be recorded (categorising them as human resource production), and given an imputed economic value.

The same should be done with those associated with direct daily personal and house maintenance activities — cooking, washing clothes, processing food ('human resource maintenance') and the range of activities such as fetching wood and water, family food farming, making items for domestic or farm use.

If the time spent by women and men on the different aspects of human resource production and maintenance is recorded in census and other statistical records, given an imputed value and shown in national accounts, considerable policy benefits accrue. For example, having a record of the amount of labour spent on the different aspects of human resource production and maintenance would highlight critical labour bottlenecks and facilitate discussion of how they are to be reduced; by direct state investment (i.e. on infrastructure), or indirect investment (i.e. providing credit for acquiring domestic technologies) or encouraging private sector involvement. Furthermore, the contribution of work in the home to socio-economic development will be put on a par with work outside it and a more balanced view achieved of the totality of economic potential in the society.

The Households: Households are generally used as the basic social and economic unit on which information in censuses and surveys is collected. However, what constitutes a household unit poses considerable conceptual problems. In large measure this is because of the conflation of the household (a residential unit) with the family (a social unit based on kinship, marriage and parenthood). To help resolve this, international guidelines have been devised which broadly define a household as a number of individuals who live together and provide the basic needs for themselves, their children and relevant others others (i.e. those who live under one roof and share a common pot). A family, on the other hand, is defined as those who are related by blood or marriage, though not necessarily living together.

Certain assumptions in fact underpin the guidelines: that households are constituted around relationships centred on marriage and parenthood, that co-residence is a defining feature, that the housing unit and the consumption unit are co-extensive, and that members of the unit pool and share economic resources. As a result many of the assumptions made about the nature of intrahousehold relations are informed by assumptions about the marriage relation itself, and by assumptions about relations between parents and children (see Roberts, 1991). Household composition in fact depends on a number of factors including rules of residence on marriage, the nature of kinship (patrilineal, matrilineal, bilineal, etc.), marriage rules (polygamy, monogamy, polyandry), inheritance rules (single, multiple or joint inheritance, post-or pre-mortem) and rules of residence for inheritors (the son destined to inherit the land may have to co-reside with his parents, unmarried siblings and his own wife and children), class (are live-in servants employed?), the availability of housing and so on.

Composition changes not only with the development cycle of the domestic group (as children are born, grow up and leave to marry or bring in their spouses and begin to have children themselves, as old people and parents age and die), but also in response to other economic, social and political factors.

Kinship still remains a politico-economic and social resource in LDCs to a much greater extent than in IMEs — providing a welfare net, a support group, and a political force — and this reflected in residential patterns and in the constantly shifting location of people residentially. As a result, the assumption that the household, particularly when viewed as an economic unit, has defined boundaries and does not overlap with others, and that people are clearly allocated to only one household unit, is invalid. Family members may sleep under one roof but neither eat together nor share a common budget; they may share a common budget but not live under the same roof; adult men, even though in recognised heterosexual relationships with specific women, may never live with them but reside in their mother's house or a men's house; some household members may share production tasks but what they produce may be consumed by other family households altogether and so on (Roberts, 1991). In much of the Caribbean, the basic set of people living together is a woman, her daughters and their children, with adult men —sons and children's fathers—spending a varied amount of time in the unit but rarely remaining stable members.

Children's fathers usually contribute something to their up-keep, but a woman maintains herself and looks to her brother as her main economic fall-back resource. Children may also be sent to live with their mother's mother or sister as much to help them as to relieve pressure on their mother's budget.

In sub-Saharan Africa, where kinship ties remain quite strong in many areas, and where polygamy is also relatively common, household composition is highly varied and complex. In urban areas a man may live in a common residence with his wife or wives, their children, some of his (or her) siblings and/or siblings' children, and members of the parental generation or their children. In the rural areas, if a man has a plurality of wives, each wife will probably have her own huts and cooking place, and will be visited by the husband in rotation.

In Latin America many men are also involved in simultaneous multiple unions but unlike sub-Saharan Africa polygamy is not legal nor officially recognised. A man may recognise one household as his main place of residence (where he keeps his working tools), but provide some economic support to two or more units, and share his time between them. A woman with children by a previous union may not be able to keep them when she joins with a second husband — they are either dispersed among her own kin or may take to living rough, joining the bands of street children found in almost all large cities (see Jelin, 1991).

In South Asia the joint family still predominates in areas of patrilineal kinship, although to a greater extent in rural than urban areas. In this system a man and his wife, their sons, wives and children, and all unmarried daughters co-reside. The patriarch is the ultimate authority in the household, and its economic head, although much of the day-to-day management may be carried out by his wife.

Inter-Household Relations: In many areas relations between households are crucial determinants of household and individual decision-making. In rural SSA all the wives of a common husband (each living in a separate hut with her children and each with her own fields, a separate budget and cooking pot) may be involved in deciding how much land to dedicate to the basic staple, or the decision may be made by the husband or the senior wife. Yet this will set the pattern of their activities for the year. Having a wife's brother in town who can sell household produce may be the crucial determinant in the decision to grow a crop, and proceeds may be divided equally. In rural India, sons may work on the family land under the direction of the father-patriarch but major production decisions may in fact be made by an absent urban-dwelling son who provides the capital needed for the inputs.

Units of production and consumption may coincide or do so only occasionally. For example, in Cameroon, Jane Guyer (1984) observed that wives produced most of the basic staples and relish crops while husbands produced an export cash crop. The women were careful to ensure they had sufficient basic household foods stocks, but also sold vegetables at the market and special delicacies to their husbands and their male kin (thus acquiring some of the men's export crop cash). Women and their children formed the production unit for staples, men and sometimes wives but usually wage labour the production unit for cocoa. Parents and children formed the basic consumption unit, but men also ate with their own matrikin.

All this points to the complexity of household composition and organisation. To make the task of identifying and measuring households manageable, especially in censuses, some simplifying assumptions are, of course, needed. However, over-simplification is misleading in circumstances where complexity prevails. In fact, many of the measurement problems that arise come from the lack of fit between diverse household characteristics and the simplified categories of household type used in censuses and national surveys. Household surveys should be able to reveal diversity and change in household composition and the relationship of this to changing socio-economic conditions.

For example, examination of the number of households with dependent children managed by a woman will throw light on female labour force participation. Collecting data on changes in household composition due to migration (of both adults and children) will throw light on labour market pressures and opportunities—and how both men and women are able to respond to them.

Household Head: Statisticians work with the convention that all households have a single authority source — the household head — despite the fact that in most societies both husband and wife have their own areas of responsibility and authority. By designating one person head of household (the reference person), census enumerators can identify all other household members in terms of their relationship to the head. However, the criteria by which to select the reference person are quite unclear. Stereotyping usually ensures that a male (not necessarily adult) is chosen whether or not he is the main source of authority. Often the census enumerator decides arbitrarily that an adult male in a household is its head, even though in reality he contributes little to family welfare (Evans, 1990).

Male headship bias leads to the underestimation of women's economic and management activities in a number of ways.

Firstly, the male chosen as household head becomes the chief respondent of census questions. But, as much research has shown, men are rarely knowledgeable about women's activities, either because of separate interests and spheres or because of cultural norms — if these dictate that women should not undertake certain activities men may turn a blind eye but are unlikely to record them. Census enumerators are not encouraged to ask women directly about their activities.

Secondly, the economic activity of the head ' is used to identify the activity status of the household as a whole irrespective of what other household members may be doing and how much income they are contributing' (Evans, 1990, p. 28).

Thirdly, in a great many households which nominally have a male head, women have complete economic responsibility, either because the men have migrated or they are unable (because of age, infirmity, etc.) to earn a livelihood.

Intra-Household Economic Relations: A major problem in policy-making is the prevalence of stereotypes in economic models of how intra-household economic relations should operate. Commonly, marriage is conceived as a partnership between two persons with reciprocal (but not necessarily equal) rights and obligations to each other, with similar rights over and obligations to the children of the marriage, and with a common set of interests. As a result, it is assumed that marriage gives rise to a unit marked by jointness of control and management of resources, and similarity or coincidence in interests and goals. Often there is a tendency to conflate household with couple, this being perhaps most marked in discussions about household resource management (see Young, 1990). Pooling and sharing are assumed to be characteristics of household economic behaviour, in large measure because marriage is supposed to create a joint domestic economy.

However, research shows that even where jointness is a social fact, the degree of economic jointness varies. In SSA there would appear to be little notion of the jointness of marital economy; in the south Asian joint family conjugal jointness is positively discouraged. In SSA where polygyny is common, an in-marrying wife is seen as a wife to the lineage rather than the male alone, and as such may be inherited on her husband's death by his actual brother or a close agnate. Wives are expected to provide for their own children and to feed their husband and his kin when necessary. While it is a husband's obligation to provide his wife/ves with the means by which they are to do this, and to provide her/them with labour at certain points in the production cycle, he is in no way obliged to maintain his wife, and indeed a woman who is a poor cultivator or cannot bear children is likely to be returned to her kin.

Where matriliny prevails, a man's obligation is as much to his mother, and his sisters and their children (who are his heirs), as to his wife: he may not even live with his wife but reside with his maternal kin, visiting her from time to time. If she lives nearby she will send food to him at his house. Elsewhere on the continent women are responsible for providing basic food and clothing for themselves and their children, while the men provide the rest. Where marriage is unstable a woman may be receiving some support for children from her ex-husband (s) or may be using her income/wage to support her 'own' children, while getting money from her present husband for the basic housekeeping and support of their children. In Latin America women try to help their mothers and sisters financially, often because they have to leave their children with them while they establish a new relationship with a man.

Where there is no concept of jointness in marriage, husband and wife may well have different strategies for survival and advancement—and sometimes these may be in opposition to each other. For example, a good deal or recent research from SSA attests to the struggles that can take place around the control of women's labour (Roberts, 1989).

A married man can call upon his wife's labour for cultivation; she may gain little or no direct benefit but none the less it is her duty as wife to assist him. The contrary does not seem to hold; that is a woman may ask her husband for assistance but usually he is rewarded by a share in the proceeds whether in the form of cooked food, or cash payment. Where men have their own crops (for example, export crops) women can expect little benefit, but wives involved in market-oriented production frequently have to give a share to the husband or indeed hand over the whole of the proceeds (a proportion being returned to them).

Studies how the variety of ways in which women attempt to capture some of their husbands' cash income as, for example, the women in Cameroon noted earlier who sell their husbands small cooked delicacies (Guyer, 1984). This pattern of independent economic activity for men and women, but mutual responsibility for children is also common in the Caribbean where a woman may have children by a number of different men, each of whom should be responsible for the upkeep of his child/ren (but not the mother). In India the joint family system reveals another pattern; all household income is given to the patriarch for redistribution among family members. There would appear to be no concept of even shares, rather sons are preferred above daughters, and eldest son above other sons. Married sons and their wives contribute their income/resources but do not necessarily get a return commensurate with their input.

What are the practical implications of these different patterns? Because of incorrect assumptions about intra-household economic relations, policies on, for example, taxation, child and marriage allowances are often misdirected and can sometimes be positively harmful. Married women in some African countries pay a higher rate of tax than their husbands because it is assumed that husbands take care of household expenses and wives' income is to cover additional or luxury expenditures. Yet the assumption of jointness is not borne out in the case of marriage goods. In many SSA countries with patrilineal kinship systems, all the property of the marriage, however acquired, belongs to the husband.

A widow can be completely dispossessed of the marital home and its contents, whether she contributed financially to their acquisition or not. To date, changes in traditional inheritance rules (i.e. customary law) have not been easy to introduce into largely male legislative bodies. In some cases, wives have taken steps to protect themselves and their children by getting husbands to agree to recognise their ownership of goods they have bought, such recognition being ratified in the presence of representatives of both sets of kin.

Even where jointness of economy is the case, questions still have to be asked about the degree to which all members of the family get equal access to its resources. Research shows that a distinction is made between the collective ('family') aspect of the budget and the personal.

Men have a far greater call on household resources than women since they can claim personal spending money as well as a share of collective resources. The 'right' of men to take household resources (whoever earned them) for personal consumption items, beer, alcohol, cigarettes, and items of conspicuous consumption (from bicycles, to dark glasses, to shoes) is much commented upon in women's accounts of domestic budgeting (Dwyer and Bruce, 1988).

Women's claims are usually confined to the collective aspect. In the poorest strata almost every where the income of each member of the family is vital to survival but often only the woman's income is entirely spent on collective consumption items.

Main Assumptions

Mainstream development economics is a version of neo-classical economics and concerns itself with the behaviour of individuals, their preferences or choices, their rationality and their self-interest. Neo-classical economics stems from the basic premises of liberal philosophy which developed in

Europe roughly at the time of the emergence of capitalist forms of production. This philosophy may have contributed to the demise of earlier forms of production but was principally concerned with the need to eradicate forms of centralised political power within society. It assumes that all human beings are capable of rationality, that they are primarily motivated by self-interest, that they make choices between competing activities in pursuit of or to maximise self-interest (i.e. choosing that action or set of actions most likely to achieve a predetermined desired goal). As a result, society operates in a relatively smooth, self-regulatory way precisely because while each person is out to maximise their own utility she has to choose goal-oriented strategies which are not in direct conflict with those of others since this may lead to inability to achieve the goal.

The role of centralised political power (the state) is to act as arbiter between irreconcilable competing interests, protecting the rights of individuals. Neo-classical economic theory focuses on markets which are assumed to be sites of free and voluntary exchange between individuals — unless both parties benefit from a transaction it will not take place. It has been said that it offers a universal theory of economic behaviour; however, it assumes the existence of markets while abstracting them from any wider institutional context.

In this world, individuals are not embedded in any thus constrained by relationships such as those of kinship or parenthood, nor are inequality, exploitation or conflict essential features.

The Household as a Corporate Unit: The theory does, of course, encompass the fact that individuals marry and bear/father children and form household units. Households are assumed to be composed of a couple and their offspring, and to allocate their labour to market and non-market work on the basis of their 'natural' comparative advantage—women specialising in motherhood and housecare, men in economic activities outside the home. Despite these natural differences, the individual tastes and preferences of spouses and other household members are lumped together so that the household is assumed to have a 'joint utility function' (a common set of goals which maximises household welfare). In other words, a simplifying assumption is made about the characteristic behaviour of the family/household: that it behaves as if it were an individual, makes choices, has tastes and preferences, and maximises utility (or welfare). It is assumed that the characteristic behaviour within the family is animated by notions of co-operation, reciprocity and sharing.

This view of the household as a corporate unit does not encourage most economists to analyse the internal structure of the household, to investigate how it actually works as a collectivity, or to enquire into the ways in which joint welfare comes to be arrived at in the interest of all family members.

Indeed, it has been argued that economics can bypass all these awkward questions by the assumption that the family is a natural unit in which sharing. reciprocity and co-operation prevail over self-interest and competition (Folbre, 1986). The family and the family-based household can thus be firmly allocated within the realm of 'the private sphere' (in contrast to the public sphere of the market), which allows them to define intra-household relations as being beyond the remit of the discipline of economics. In this model it is assumed that the basic form of household survival is through selling labour on the market. However, in most LDCs the majority of households are also family-based enterprises, producing not only for the market but for their own consumption as well. Production decisions have to aim to reach a balance between market and non-market activities.

The main problem in analysing this behaviour for economists lies in the fact that relations between household-enterprises and the economy cannot be defined in terms of market forces alone (Evans, 1991). To cope with this a specific branch of economics was developed to provide better tools and concepts for understanding such economic behaviour — the New Household Economics (NHE).

The Household as a Decision-Making Unit: Becker (1965) argues that the household as an economic entity behaves in a way analogous to the firm. It makes both production and consumption decisions which are guided by the need to minimise the costs of production and maximise family consumption. Labour is deployed in response to various pressures: differences in cost or effort between producing something at home as against buying it; the difference between the wage that a household member could get on the market as against the cost of replacing the services/activities foregone within the household (the opportunity cost of labour); and the price of goods.

Becker links the family as a 'natural' kinship unit, motivated by co-operation and sharing, and the household as an enterprise, operating much as the neo-classical theory of the firm predicts. His household is, however, clearly situated within a capitalist market economy; it is bound into markets for labour and goods/services and influenced by prices therein. But his analogy between household and firm is very strained since many exchanges between household members cannot be compared to those involved in buying and selling in the market and many activities cannot simply be dropped because another acitivity is more profitable (Evans, 1989).

There are other problems with the theory. What justifies the assumption that husband and wife share tastes/ preferences? If behaviour within the market is characterised by natural selfishness (or self-interest) yet in the family selflessness (or altruism) naturally prevails, is there not a problem of theoretical coherence (see Folbre, 1986)? In other words, are human beings by nature somewhat schizophrenic? How are we to understand both relations of conflict and competition and those of sharing and reciprocity? 'Traditional models of price theory and market behaviour are silent on the family. When the silence is broken the old myths and views turn out to be very insecure. While they can be preserved by some special — and typically far-fetched — assumptions, that is hardly the way to face a real challenge' (Sen, 1983, p. 25).

The curious contradiction between presumption of self-interest as the principal motivator of market behaviour, enabling the efficient allocation of resources within it, and of altruism within the family, ensuring the efficient allocation of familial resources, appears to have troubled Becker. In later works on the family influenced by the then recent theories of sociobiology, he suggests that the paterfamilias acts as a benevolent dictator to ensure that every family member acts in the interests of the collectivity (Becker, 1976).

This poses another puzzle in that, according to this model, husbands, despite their economic power, do not act as selfish tyrants, whereas children (and wives) despite their economic powerlessness apparently do. In other words, the model is based on a rather odd prediction of the likely outcome of unequal power relations. But then relations between individuals are not, according to Becker, relations of power, least of all those between husband and wife. In this he differs from John K. Galbraith who has a much clearer view: 'The household, in the established economics, is essentially a disguise for the exercise of male authority' (Galbraith, 1973). From the point of view of analysing household behaviour in LDCs the assumption in the NHE approach of fully-developed market economy presents serious difficulties. Some of these have been subsequently dealt with by other economists. Allan Low, influenced by the work of the Russian economist Chayanov (1966), for example, showed the need to include both market and non-market opportunities in his analysis of the economic behaviour of farm-households in LDCs (Low, 1986). He showed that factors such as household composition (including the ratio of workers (adults) to consumers (children, elders and adults), and the household division of labour, were important as were differences in labour force participation of all household members (see Evans, 1990). Low uses the logic of comparative advantage to explain the different allocation of labour but does not address the question of possible conflict of interests between different household or family members. In this sense his vision does not greatly differ from that of orthodox neo-classical economists. Yet research into intra-household relations show that conflict of interest as much as convergence inevitably occur over labour allocation and the distribution of other resources within the family-based household.

Theories on Human Nature

Studying the household and trying to make sense of observed organisational and behavioural patterns almost inevitably raises questions about the correctness of assumptions as to universal and unchanging human nature. Have neoclassical economics and liberal philosophy got it right — are human beings primarily motivated by individual self-interest? Or do the values of co-operation and reciprocity play as prominent a part in humankind's make up? Anthropologists would argue that the evidence shows that both co-operation and competition, altruism and self-interest, are potential forms of behaviour, and that the way in which the economy is organised plays a key role in whether individualism and self-interest predominate, or co-operation and altruism. Most previous forms of social organisation have not encouraged the pursuit of economic self-interest in the way or to the extent capitalism does.

Indeed, tendencies to economic differentiation were often culturally proscribed (witchcraft accusations being one means of preventing marked economic differentiation), or certain social mechanisms ensured that those who succeeded economically gained social prestige by giving their wealth away, often in grand displays of conspicuous but collective consumption. New analytical tools are badly needed which will allow us to develop theories of co-operative behaviour which can be compared to those of self-interest so as to see which have more predictive power. Economics appears to be alone among the social sciences in largely discounting the importance of the ways in which individuals are embedded in social structures, the ways in which a variety of institutions, including the family, shape appropriate behaviour towards others; and how these are different for boys and girls, with ideas about masculinity and femininity playing a strong part in defining appropriate behaviour, preferences and expectations.

Women are socialised from very early on to be more selfless than men, less personally ruthless, less experimental and daring. Boys may be socialised to behave in ways which appear completely counter to the dictates of self-interest. Furthermore, cultural conditions also shape individuals' responses to given situations — many jokes turn upon the differing responses of people from different cultures to the same situation. Studying the household also makes one question the stereotypes built into the way we see the world; to stand back from the ideological representation of the family as the supportive bulwark in a heartless world, to ask what relations between men and women are like in reality, what underpins them, what transforms or distorts them. Rather than seeing these relations as effects of unchanging human nature, or of set patterns of roles, they can be seen as dynamic and changing, with men and women bargaining with each other as they seek to further their own advancement as well as the collective good. As David Sahn puts it 'there is a need to determine... how household members with divergent preference orderings reconcile their differences through some sort of bargaining process' (Sahn, 1985, p. 16). A number of analysts have looked at household dynamics in terms of bargaining theory.

Amartya Sen (1985, 1987) suggests that the intra-couple dynamic is most usefully represented as one of *co-operative conflict*.

He constructs a model which he suggests is widely applicable. In this, there are a number of potential solutions (he calls them collusive agreements) to differences of goals and strategies, the one finally adopted being the result of the bargaining ability of individuals. Ability, however, in this sense is not a personal negotiating skill: while household members may have divergent views on how to invest resources, use labour and so on, they do not all come with equal power to the bargaining table.

One important component in bargaining power is the perception of self-worth, which differs widely between family members (particularly men and women), and which influences perceptions of advantage and legitimacy. This is based in part on the 'perceived contribution' that the various household members make to household well-being. In modern society, two factors enter here: actual ability to earn income or bring valued resources into the household, and the value given to different members' contributions. As we have seen, since men often get privileged access to income-earning opportunities, and women's contribution to both household and external labour is generally underrated, the idea that the person providing the main inputs to the family or society should make the decisions as to resource allocation is reinforced in men's favour. Sen's concept of co-operative conflict nicely captures what I have noted above as a more realistic interpretation of human behaviour: the mixture of cooperation and competition, of seeking own aims and furthering those of others. His analysis points to the need to be aware of the factors which throw the relation out of equilibrium and balance into one of inequality.

Sen argues that a number of forces have conspired against women's bargaining position over time and that: 'Asymmetries — however developed — are stable and sustained, and the relative weakness of women in co-operative conflict in one period tends to sustain relative weakness in the next' (Sen, 1985, p. 13).

Planning with and for Women

Once families are brought into economic analysis explicitly, a variety of questions of economic theory and policy emerge (Sen, 1983, p. 26).

The nature of economic models and concepts, the tendency to aggregation and to making simplifying assumptions, make it all too easy to exclude women's activities and contributions. We have also looked at the ways in which statisticians, who provide the data with which planners and economists work, are hampered in producing a better picture of reality, because of assumptions and stereotypes built into their conceptual models. As a result many of the most dynamic processes taking place in LDCs cannot be captured numerically, and women's economic contributions fail to gain proper recognition. People concerned with developing policies which build on women's social and economic contributions to society as well as to the family face another major obstacle. There is a contradiction between what has been called the seamless web of women's lives and the compartmentalised and gendered mode of conventional thinking about society and social processes in general.

Thus, for example, the conceptual separation between the public and the private, productive and unproductive activity, between work and home does not accurately reflect women's reality. It is a male perspective. Linkages need to be made conceptionally between various aspects of women's experience: between family and employment, between unpaid work and paid work, between production and reproduction. So too the link must be made between the production and maintenance of people, and the capacity of an economy to produce goods and services for a variety of markets. We have also argued that economic theory still cannot help us understand the interlock between household as family and as enterprise and the economy. Since household enterprise are very widespread in LDCs, particularly among the poorer strata, policy instruments are needed which will support these enterprises.

Support for poor households is essential both for economic growth and the relief of poverty. But policy-makers need to know under what conditions they operate as bounded units, and when they do not, what the wider aggregation are; they need to know what the major constraints to economic viability are — labour, inputs, markets, credit, training, and which household members are the key operators, entrepreneurs or managers. They also need to know what work women do in the market and in the household, how the two interconnect, and what influences women's ability to participate in economic activity. They also need to understand the time-constraints under which women operate and ask questions about whether increased paid labour force participation is at the cost of unpaid household work or (already scarce) leisure time.

When they see that women are moving out of one type of activity and into another they need to know to what extent this reflects a shift from part-time to full-time work, from temporary to permanent employment or vice versa; whether the shift is complementary to or in conflict with trends in male employment (Evans, 1990).

They need to know too whether these shifts are long- or short-term and if the former what additional services need to be provided to women to ensure stability of availability. Further, they need to know about intra-household distribution of income. Some information is gathered on income but, as Baster (1981) points out, information on income is in fact often missing from macro-level data; when it does appear it tends to refer to households' total monthly and annual cash income, regardless of source. Reliance on money income leads to distortions given the importance in many LDCs of payment in kind and the production of goods for own consumption.

Source of income can also be relevant, particularly if there is extensive reliance on transfers from kin or the state. Lastly, little information is given on the control of the various factors determining access to actual or potential income: land, labour, credit, training and paid employment, or to the extent to which the person earning an income controls it.

Given the lack of jointness of marriage as an economic relation, a wide range of policy measures need to be rethought. It may be useful to do this by conceptualising the relations between men and women within the family as characterised by co-operative conflict as we have outlined above.

Because of women's weak access to personal money, their greater commitment to and dependence on the collective aspect of the household fund, and the constraints on their ability to build up assets despite their entrepreneurial skills and vocation, policy-makers need to consider ways to strengthen the collective aspect of household resources, as much as to support women's enterprises. The aim should not be to reinforce women's dependence, but to enhance the interdependence of men and women to the benefit of both.

Obviously, the foregoing discussion puts ample light on different concepts and assumptions for women resource development. This may enlighten the development practitioners a lot. Similar further researches can discover new lods and techniques which can be instrumental in utilising the vast potential of women resource in big and appropriate way.

8

Developing Professionalism Among Women

> "The truth is that for everything that can be accomplished by showing a person when he is wrong, ten times as much can be accomplished by showing him where he is right. The reason we don't do it so often is that it's more fun to throw a rock through a window than to put in a pane of glass."
>
> —*Robert T. Allen*

Developing the art of professionalism is an important aspect of human resource development. Here in this chapter we will try to elucidate the origin and growth of professionalism among women which necessary for turning them into a vast pool of active human resource, practically.

First we shall put light on 'profession' and 'professionalism'.

Most of the scholars whether economists, sociologists or social scientists, are confused while defining the term 'profession'. According to Rueschemeyer "The term profession denotes service occupations that apply a systematic body of knowledge to problems which are highly relevant to central values of the society." A.M. Carr-Saunders and P.A. Wilson claim in their classic study 'The Professions' that "the typical profession exhibits a complex of characteristics, and that other vocations approach this condition more or less closely, owing to the profession of some of these characteristics fully or partially developed." This complex of characteristics is professionalism.

Morris Logan defines: "A profession is vocation whose practice is founded upon an understanding of the theoretical structure of some department of learning or science and upon the ability accompanying such understanding. This understanding and these abilities are applied to the vital practical affairs of man. The profession¼ considers its first ethical imperative to be altruistic service to the client."

Remarkably, in primitive societies man was the food gatherer. It is through hunting that he used to get animal flesh. It was immaterial for the women whether he faced danger while hunting or not, for he was duty-bound to provide food for his family members. The woman had to stay in her dwelling—cave or igloo—to protect her children. She and her children were dependents upon the 'brave and god-like male, who had to provide food at his own risk. She was thus not only a dependent but also a 'helper', an automatic subordinate. She used to dress the products of the hunt, cooked meat and fish, preserved skins for clothing and warmth, greeted her mate with joy when he was successful, starved along with her children if he was not.

She was never a participant. The survival of such races was critically dependent upon the man's skill and courage. But with the advent of cultivation, it has become compulsory on the part of women to participate in the outdoor work. As such, she used to take part in some of the agricultural operations like weeding, transplanting and harvesting in the fields and in every other type of work that she could. Even today, women labours constitute more than half of the total agricultural force.

The Japanese anthropologists noted in 1930s that female status was comparatively higher amongst the poorer families since their women worked as agricultural labourers, made winnowing baskets, and did embroidery work. The women's labour force increased during the 19th century and from the early period of 20th century due to the upliftment of women from the tradition-bound ethos drought alout by the influence of the various social reforms of successive periods. The two World Wars compelled women to participate in the occupations, which were the monopoly of men. The industrial employment of women including those who were married was a fairly widespread phenomenon in the 19th century. It was during the first rationing system in 1943 that middle class women stepped out *en masse* to serve in the offices, though, previously, there were few women teachers, doctors and nurses.

The participation of women in labour market can be seen as consisting of two streams. The first occurring during the industrialisation and connected with the generally low level of wages, consists of women who have to supplement the family economically by accepting gainful employment. After industrial revolution more and more women took to working, while, before this, the only work the women considered suitable for was the sale of their bodies.

Remarkably, Industrial revolution caused to develop sources of conflicts between the two sexes. The shift of the most lucrative economic activity out of the home into the factory had a number of effects. Due to the child bearing and rearing responsibility of women, the man was usually first to leave the home, and factory products soon displaced home produced goods in the market economy. The growth of the modern economy meant that the man became the principal source of income within the family.

And as traditional society began to crumble, money income became an important source of social status. Thus, not only did the economic activities of the sexes become physically separated, but the social value of the man's activities measured in terms of money, became separated from his wife's.

Because household economic activity was not given a market value, a woman had no way left before her to achieve economic status independent of her husband. Hence, she had to join the labour force for earning. The technological changes of the industrial revolution transformed the processes of production. As a result, the women of the urban proletariat and many of the artisan groups were drawn into the factories, mills and mines as unskilled wage earners. The majority of women found it necessary to work outside the home to augment the family income. Increased cost of living necessitated the supplementary earnings to the chief wage earnings and it was deemed preferable that the daughters also should work for wages. At the same time, industry seeking to keep down costs of production in order to keep up profits, offered only this supplementary wages to the daughters.

Women thus came to occupy the position of marginal workers in the new economy. The employment of women in industrial nations has thus been a development arising neither from social requirement of women's work in industries nor from a women's inherent need for work, but was mainly caused by the desire of entrepreneurs to utilise cheap labour for profit making purposes.

Norably, during the World War II, women entered the labour force due to dire economic necessity and feelings of patriotism and for the first time, experienced the financial and psychological independence that an income activity outside the home could afford. Raising cost of living also meant that more families could afford to send their female children to high schools and colleges. These women, better educated than their mothers, were attracted towards labour force by the possibility of higher pay.

Thus during 1960s, there was a unprecedented increase in number of women with small children with jobs. Economic pressures aggravated by inflation and the demands of a higher standard of living, push women into the work force, but they are often not free to accept the best jobs at the best rate. Convenience of locations limit their choice.

However, transformation of women's work, has been the result of much more than the advancement of industry and trade. Development of science and technology, changes in attitudes and aspirations, in social structures and family living patterns have all concurred to relieve the burden of motherhood. Many women today serve gainful employment not because they are all educated but because they face economic strains and because wife's income is considered essential to the family standard of living. The attitude prevails that woman only supplements the family income and can afford to take less.

Furthermore, an equally or more qualified and hard working educated woman does not mind to work in the lower rate of vocation than man; hence, employers prefer employing women whenever possible, as they get less for more work. With the active encouragement for the women education in India, by the Government, after Independence and the increased opportunities for potential jobs in industrial and domestic spheres than white-collar jobs, women are constrained to take part in the labour force.

The demographic and technological progresses have reduced the time span of child rearing in relation to the life cycle and alleviated the burden of housework, and women started to get fulfilment outside the home. Highly educated women are likely to be more interested in the employment, but by far, the largest number of women work to support families and to contribute their pay to the family income to lift it above the poverty level. Leading educational officers in the Israeli defence forces emphasise that the presence of girls in the army is responsible for the polite atmosphere among soldiers. Throughout the world, women are in the working force who earn monthly salary.

In South-East Asia, commerce is open to women. In Jakarta, wives of senior civil servants run shops and make jewellery. In Thailand many large hotels are run by women. Philippine women are adept in real estate business as stock brokers and runners of business.

Now, women have entered into the technical field, medical, teaching and nursing. They are working as pilots, taxi drivers, policewomen, ambassadors, ministers and heads of nations. They are serving in territorial army of Israel and most difficult and dangerous job of espionage, etc.

Way back, Nehru wrote, "I invariably think of a prison and a zoo. How can a nation go ahead if half of its population is kept away in a kind of prison? Tear the *Purdah* and let each one of us see the light of the day."

Remarkably, in this modern age women are mainly entering into the lucratively paid jobs to enhance the family income and prestige and to utilise the education and the social status, rather than merely due to the economic constraints. The study of Kapur also states that educated urban women have now begun to realise that job can raise their self-esteem and self-confidence and can accomplish their socio-psychological security and freedom.

The various studies and surveys as well as statistics show that educated women are now more keen and desirous of utilising their education and training than was the case previously. The desire to seek escape from the monotony and dullness of home life drives quitc a number of women into the employment market. Women began to work with different motives, some wanted to occupy themselves mentally and make their education purposeful, some began to work just to get rid of boredom, while some others do so because of their interest in a particular vocation and a large number due to economic pressure.

Some women may have to work, when permanent of temporary inadequacy like sudden death of father, husband or some other earning member of the family occurs. Today, working wives show no strong internal commitment to work. They work for variety of reasons including the need to feel useful and important—but they work mainly in order to earn money which they do not absolutely need.

It is pertinent to note that in India, most of the women seek outside jobs to a great extent due to economic necessity. Some take up a profession to kill boredom, for they have more leisure now than women had in olden days. The present trend suggests that women in greater number are threatening to enter the man's exclusive domain and remunerative employment. It is essentially the middle class women, who have forged forth into the employment market.

The women are taking to work to utilise their potentialities in addition to fulfilling the functions as wife and mother.

Some are for adult, companionships or for personal independence. Some may find their home making tasks dull or unrewarding. Some for fruitful use of their spare time and others might have originally planned to resume the careers; yet others, who have trained themselves to be teachers or nurses may be impelled to return to work to make use of professional skills. Some may feel that their lives will be empty when their children are grown and no longer live with them. Such women try to enter into professions.

Most women crave for higher standard of living in their families. Much of their earnings go to refurnishing and redecorating their homes with domestic appliances, nutritious food, pocket money and toys for the children. The author of the present study also observed working women at their work place chitchatting about the modern gadgets to be purchased for their families like TV, grinder, mixy, tape recorder, etc. Families with working women as members spend their extra money for the luxuries, in order to exhibit and enhance high style life in their respective areas. Some women assert against the traditional women roles. If the women were given the same opportunities which man have had, the progress of humanity would have been doubled. Why all women should cook? It is not biological. It is working socially to the advantage of man. We can tell cross-culturally that all men can work and also look after children as well. Women can take up any modern job which men can, with the same ease and efficiency.

But in the modern society, the occupational role of women is merely extension of her sexual sides. The sector of employment open to women workers is often an air hostess and no one is surprised at seeing her travel to far corners of the earth.

Office women are working for gross economic necessity and to enhance the family/husband's income. Whereas women medical staff are for independent income, to serve the people, to utilise the education and they also need status in the society. They are working not merely for the economic reason like that of office staff. Even teaching staff also are not career minded fully for the economic reasons but for supplementing the family income, ambition of career and independent income.

Until 1950s, husband would expect his wife to welcome him with smiling face at the entrance of the house with water in her hand and children waiting for dad in the evening when he comes back from office. When he looks at his wife with smiling face he feels relieved of all the troubles and frustration of the day. He prefers to have such women as life mate. But, now it has reversed and the children wait for both the parents because woman is also working.

It is often observed that an individual's background plays a significant role in the formation of his attitudes and beliefs. His family, school, neighbourhood, level of education, type of occupation and the income—all determine to a great extent, the type and quality of his attitudes and values.

A syndrome of these attitudes and values determine the level of modernity achieved by an individual in society. In other words, we may say that the level of modernity that an individual has in society depends largely on the character of his socio-demographic factors. For the purpose of analysis, we are treating the position of the individual here as a dependent variable and background characteristics like education, occupation and income, as independent variables. "Modernity is the result of an interplay of a complex number of factors like the rural-urban residence, spread of literacy, and employment in a formal bureaucratic organisation. These individual background attributes help in determining the level of individual modernity." Attitudes determine the role played by an individual. In turn, role of an individual determines the attitudes and the opinions towards a particular aspect.

"Since the attitudes of a person are central to his subjective life and largely determine his thoughts, feelings and behaviours, it is very significant to know the attitudes of a group of persons and, more so, the changes taking place in attitudes, if one wants to study the social change or the direction towards which the society is moving."

In the earlier periods, women were only housewives and helpmates. They were dependents on their husbands. Providing food and economic obligations were the duties of male. But times have changed. Due to the advent of education—that is the modern western education—job oriented and professional degrees, the attitude of women also changed. Having acquired the preferred education, they cannot sit idle in the houses, as an economic obligation on the part of the husband. Women too want to utilise their education and talent which they have earned through education and vocational training. Hence, they have taken to out-of-home gainful vocation and they are now the bread earners of their families.

Though women could get education and later on, employment, were subject to change in their attitudes, beliefs and behaviour in the direction of modernity. The education and the employment of women, in turn, change her attitudes and opinions on the social aspects of various institutions such as marriage, family, education, customs, etc. Economic aspect plays an important role in determining the attitudes of an individual.

The purchasing power is determined depending on one's economic capability. The mere improvement of purchasing capacity is the change of one's behaviour towards modernity. Economic aspect plays an important role in determining the opinions and attitudes of an individual. Three different economic categories of working women are selected for the study. Inkeles finds education as the most important of the influences moving men from 'traditionalism' to 'modernity' in developing countries.

Again he finds that, "A man's occupational experience emerges as one of the strongest variables in explaining a person's modernity. Summing up, he mentions that educational and occupational experience and urbanism maintain an absolute and relative strength of their impact on modernisation, despite great variations in the culture of man undergoing such an experience, meaning thereby that, micro-structural forces have great power to shape attitudes, values and behaviour in a regular way within a wide variety of macro-structural settings."

Keeping in view the immense importance of their social variables, it was presumed in our study that a positive relationship between background characteristics and the change of attitudes and opinions would exist. We hypothesise here that the more educated and higher the income of the respondent, the higher will be her score on the level of change of attitudes. Since the women are not generally considered to be the bread winners of the family, and they take employment mostly to supplement and support the family income, it was thought pertinent here to see if the total family income of the respondents also had any relationship with the level of modernity. It is the total family income which really determines the purchasing power of the family and socio-economic strata of society to which they belong and, it is the very socio-economic group which moulds an individual's attitudes, beliefs and behaviours.

Therefore, it was assumed that individual's modernisation not only depends on an individual's own income but also on the total family income. In other words, we may say that, the higher the income of the family, the higher the level of change in their opinions.

Again `Income' determines attitudes and opinions of the individual, that too, the income of the family determines the greater part of one's opinions. Hence, the respondents were distributed according to the level of income of the family. The income of the family determines the position of the individual within it. Teaching staff are better placed in the income than the office staff, where medical staff are still better placed than the other two. That is due to the difference in the occupations/positions of their respective roles. It is hypothesised that the higher the income of one's family, the higher the attitudinal changes in their lives.

Further, it was thought to distribute the respondents age-wise. Because, age of the individual also plays an important role in the changing status towards modernisation. Status generally correlates with the age of the individual because a woman born before the Independence is less modern than the woman born after the Independence.

A person born in the 1950s is less modern than the person born during 1990s. A woman born before Independence was traditional because she was brought up during the colonial days of seclusions, segregation and was less educated, whereas woman born after Independence has been brought up in the democratic, secular and socialistic society. She has been given freedom to move in the society. She has more facilities for education and so on. A person born during 1990s is much more modern than the person born during 1940s because of the educational and vocational opportunities provided in the society. Hence, age of the individual is a significant factor in determining one's changes towards modernity.

Both marital status of an individual and the level of change correlates with each other. With the marriage of a maiden, she may have to change with the new environment and adjust to the prevailing conditions of that new atmosphere. While adjusting to the new position, her attitudes and opinions are also subject to change. Hence, it is decided to distribute the subjects according to the marital status of an individual.

As such, we can infer that the higher the caste of the individual, the higher the level of change, the lower the caste of the individual, the lower the level of change in their attitudes. Hence, caste barrier plays very important role in determining one's level of change in his outlook and attitudes.

"Since India is full of cultural complexities, contradictions, and regional variations, what may stand true for urban India, may not stand true for rural India. Hence, it was thought pertinent to cross-tabulate the data area-wise, where the subjects spent maximum period of their life.

Thus it can safely be surmised that the attitudinal change may be more among the urban respondents than the rural respondents. That may be due to the cultural differences between village and town. Hence, it is assumed that the level of change may be more in the urban than in the rural respondents. Prolonged association with the rural environment make them less modern.

REFERENCES

Altbach, Edith Hoshino, *Women in America,* D.C. Heath and Co., 1974.

Baig, Tara Ali, *India's women power,* S. Chand and Co. (P) Ltd., New Delhi, 1976.

Chapman, Jane Roberts, *Economic independence for women: The foundation for equal rights,* Vol. I, Sage Publications, 1976.

Dandiya, C.K. (ed.); *Women in Rajasthan;* University of Rajasthan; 1975.

Davis, Delia, *Woman-work,* Oxford University Press, 1976.

Hate, C.A., *Changing status of women in post-independence India,* Allied Publishers, 1969.

Huber, Joan (ed.), *Changing women and changing society,* The University of Chicago; 1973.

Kapur, Promilla, *Marriage and the working women in India,* Vikas Publishing House, 1970.

Kapur, Promilla, *The changing status of the working women in India,* Vikas Publishing House, 1974.

Mitchell, Duncan, G. (ed.), *The dictionary of sociology,* Routledge and Kegan Paul, 1968, p. 138.

Myrdal, Alva and Kelin, Viola, *Women's two roles: Home and Work,* Routledge and Kegan Paul, 1956, p. 42.

Nanda, B.R. (ed.), *Indian women from purdah to modernity,* Vikas Publishing House, 1976, p. 12.

Ramanamma, S., *Graduate employed women in an urban setting, Dastane* Ramanamma and Co., Poona, 1979.

Ranade, S.N. and Ramachandran P., *Women and employment,* Bombay, Tata Institute of Social Sciences, 1970.

Reddy, Kumari, *Problems of married working women with particular reference to Tirupati,* Thesis submitted for M.Sc. Home Science, S.V. University, Tirupati, 1972.

Sethi, Raj Mohini, *Modernisation of working women in developing societies,* National Publishing House, 1976.

Smuts, Robert, W., *Woman and work in America,* Columbia University Books Inc., 1959.,

Smuts, Robert, W., *Women and work in America,* Columbia University Books Inc., 1959.

9

Beijing Declaration (1995)

Many conferences, committees and covenants have been held at national, regional and international level for empowering women and transform them into useful human resource. To curb the discrimination, enhance educational level and ameliorate other unjust practices have been their main objective.

Beijing Declaration (1995) is a landmark in this direction. Hence we are reproducing the text of Beijing Declaration in this chapter.

1. We, the Government participating in the Fourth World Conference of Women.

2. Gathered here in Beijing in September 1995, the year of the fiftieth anniversary of the founding of the United Nations.

3. Determined to advance the goals of equality, development and peace for all women everywhere in the interest of all humanity.

4. Acknowledging the voices of all women everywhere and taking note of the diversity of women and their roles and circumstances, honouring the women who paved the way and inspired by the hope present in the world's youth.

5. Recognise the status of women has advanced in some important respects in the past decade but that progress has been uneven, inequalities between women and men have persisted and major obstacles remain, with serious consequences for the well-being of all people.

6. Also recognise that this situation is exacerbated by the increasing poverty that is affecting the lives of the majority of the world's people in particular women and children, with origins in both the national and international domains.

7. Dedicate ourselves unreservedly to addressing these constraints and obstacles and thus enhancing further the advancement and empowerment of women all over the world, and agree that this requires urgent action in the spirit of determination, hope, cooperation and solidarity now and to carry us forward into the next century.

We reaffirm our commitment to:

8. The equal rights nd inherent human dignity of women and men and other purposes and principles enshrined in the Charter of the United Nations, to the Universal Declaration of Human Rights and other international human rights instruments, in particular the Convention on the Elimination of All Forms of Discrimination against Women and the Convention on the Rights of the Child, as well as the Declaration on the Elimination of violence against Women and the Declaration on the Right to Development.

9. Ensure the full implementation of the human rights of women and of the girl child as an inalienable, integral and indivisible part of all human rights and fundamental freedoms.

10. Build on consensus and progress made at previous

United Nations Conferences and summits—on women in Nairobi in 1985, on children in new York in 1990, on environment and development in Rio de Janeiro in 1992, on human rights, in Vienna in 1993, on population and development in Cairo in 1994 and on social development in Copenhagen in 1995 with the objective of achieving equality, development and peace.

11. Achieve the full and effective implementation of the Nairobi Forward-looking Strategies for the Advancement of Women.

12. The empowerment and advancement of women, including the right to freedom of thought, conscience, religion and belief, thus contributing men, individually or in community with others and thereby guaranteeing them the possibility of realising their full potential in society and shaping their lives in accordance with their own aspirations.

We are convinced that:

13. Women's empowerment and their full participation on the basis of equality in all spheres of society, including participation in the decision-making process and to power, are fundamental for the achievement of equality, development and peace.

14. Women's rights are human rights.

15. Equal rights, opportunities and access to resources, equal sharing of responsibilities for the family by men and women, and a harmonious partnership between them are critical to their well-being and that of their families as well as the consolidation of democracy.

16. Eradication of poverty based an sustained economic growth, social development, environmental protection and social justice requires the involvement of women in economic

and social development, equal opportunities and the full and equal participation of women and men as agents and beneficiaries of people-centred sustainable development.

17. The explicit recognition and reaffirmation of the right of all women to control all aspects of their health, in particular their own fertility, is basic to their empowerment.

18. Local national, regional and global peace is attainable and is inextricably linked with the advancement of women, who are a fundamental force for leadership, conflict resolution and the promotion of lasting peace at all levels.

19. It is essential to design, implement and monitor, with the full participation of women, effective, efficient and mutually reinforcing gender-sensitive policies and programmes including development policies and programmes, at all levels that will foster the empowerment and advancement of women.

20. The participation and contribution of all actors of civil society, particularly women's groups and networks and other non-governmental organisations and community-based organisations, with full respect for their autonomy, in cooperation with Governments and the international community recognise the need to take priority action for the empowerment and advancement of women.

We are determined to:

22. Intensify efforts and actions to achieve the goals of the Nairobi Forward-looking Strategies for the Advancement of Women by the end of this century.

23. Ensure the full enjoyment by women and the girl child of all human rights and fundamental freedoms and take effective action against violations of these rights and freedoms.

24. Take all necessary measures to eliminate all forms of discrimination against women and the girl child and remove all obstacles to gender equality and the advancement and empowerment of women.

25. Encourage men to participate fully in all actions towards equality.

26. Promote women's economic independence, including employment and eradicate the persistent and increasing burden of poverty on women by addressing the structural causes of poverty through changes in economic structures, ensuring equal access for all women, including those in rural areas, as vital development agents to productive resources, opportunities and public services.

27. Promote people-centred sustainable development, including sustained economic growth, through the provision of basic education, life long education, literacy and training, and primary health care for girls and women.

28. Take positive steps to ensure peace for the advancement of women and, recognising the leading role that women have played in the peace movement, work actively towards general and complete disarmament under strict and effective international control, and support negotiations on the conclusion, without delay of a universal and multilaterally and effectively verifiable comprehensive nuclear-test ban treaty which contributes to nuclear disarmament and the prevention of the proliferation of nuclearn weapons in all its aspects.

29. Prevent and eliminate all forms of violence against women and girls.

30. Ensure equal access to and equal treatment of women and men in education and health care and enhance women's sexual reproductive health as well as education.

31. Promote and protect all human rights of women and girls.

32. Intensify efforts to ensure equal enjoyment of all human rights and fundamental freedoms for all women and girls who face multiple barriers to their empowerment and advancement because of such factors as their race, age, language, ethnicity, culture, religion or disability or because they are indigenous people.

33. Ensure respect for international law, including humanitarian law, in order to protect women and girls in particular.

34. Develop the fullest potential of girls and women of all ages, ensure their full and equal participation in building a better world for all and enhance their role in the development process.

We are determined to:

35. Ensure women's equal access to economic resources, including land, credit, science and technology, vocational training, information, communication and markets, as a means to further the advancement and empowerment of women and girls, including through the enhancement of their capacities to enjoy the benefits of equal access to these resources, inter alia by means of international cooperation.

36. Ensure the success of the Platform for Action, which will require a strong commitment on the part of Governments, international organisations and institutions at all levels. We are deeply convinced that economic development, social development and environmental protection are interdependent and mutually reinforcing components of sustainable development, which is the framework for our efforts to achieve a higher quality of life

for all people. Equitable social development that recognises empowering the poor, particularly women living in poverty, to utilise environmental resources for sustainable development. We also recognise that broadbased and sustained economic growth in the context of sustainable development is necessary to sustain social development and social justice. The success of the Platform for Action will also require adequate mobilisation of resources at the national and international levels as well as new and additional resources to the developing countries from all available funding mechanisms, including multilateral, bilateral and private sources for the advancement of women; financial resources to strengthen the capacity of national, sub-regional, regional and international institutions, a commitment to equal rights, equal responsibilities and equal opportunities and to the equal participation of women and men in all national, regional and international bodies and policy-making processes; and the establishment or strengthening of mechanisms at all levels for accountability to the world's women.

37. Ensure also the success of the Platform for Action in countries with economies in transition, which all require continued international cooperation and assistance;

38. We hereby adopt and commit ourselves as Governments to implement the following Platform for Action, ensuring that a gender perspective is reflected in all our policies and programmes. We urge the United Nations system, regional and international financial institutions other relevant regional and international institutions and all women and men, as well as non-governmental organisation, with full respect for their autonomy, and all actors of civil society, in cooperation with Governments, to fully commit themselves and contribute to the implementation of this Platform for Action.

10

Role of Liberation

> "We must keep in the forefront of our minds the fact that whenever we take away the liberties of those whom we hate, we are opening the way to loss of liberty for those we love."
>
> —*Wendell L. Willkie*

As the famous adage goes man is born free but he is bound in chains everywhere. Freedom and liberty are necessary prerequisites of proper growth and development of human personality. Women are considered subservient to men in all societies in more or lesser degrees.

Here we intend to discuss role of liberty in women resource development.

In act, the women's liberation movement has created an interest amongst all kinds of people all over the world to find out more about women and the different types of roles they are playing. Women in the past had been given some traditional roles based on custom, nature and culture. They were confined to their family and household affairs. Thus the traditional society is responsible for the damage done to their personality development.

Women's liberation does not have an immediate relevance

to the Indian social situation. It is the product of an urbanised middle class with a large number of women trained in professions, as a result of expanding educational opportunities, whose professional skills are wasted by their having to limit themselves to domestic work. 'It relates to the crisis in the concept of domestic work being somehow inferior both in terms of human intelligence and the use of labour and energy. Thus for women's liberation we have either to raise the status of domestic work to bring it at per with other professional works, or else through a highly mechanised system, the energy and intelligence spent on cooking and cleaning will have to be drastically reduced. It also relates to the changing situation of the family as a component of society in a developed industrial system, where the women ceases to be essentially only the procreator of children and the property of her husband.

The significance of the movement to the Indian scene is that by radicalising the analysis of the role of women in society, it has introduced a number of fresh perspectives to our understanding of women and society. 'Women's Liberation', therefore, refers to a high level of education in women, freedom to enter any type of occupational field, marriage not being a necessity, not covering the head in front of in-laws after marriage, believing in sex relation before marriage, wearing any 'mod' dress other than sari, going to parties and dances alone, not depending on man, keeping servants in the house, possessing different types of electrical appliances, giving sex education to children, being against dominating family members, and disliking interference in their private life.

The women herself must get rid of 'ghosts', refuse to live in a 'doll's house' and to be treated as a sex-commodity. She has to liberate herself as an individual person. There has been the positive aspect of liberation, together with the negative one, that is—liberation from oppression, exploitation and discrimination. The positive aspect says—liberation into happiness and self-fulfilment, not as a women apart from men, but as woman living with man, with equal rights and obligations.

Education

In ancient India women were by and large educated. Parents were often anxious to have scholarly daughter born in their families; ordinary well-to-do families could hardly have neglected the education of girls. Upanayana ritual was also obligatory for them and this must have ensured in giving a certain amount of Vedic and literary education to all the girls in the Brahmana, Kshatriya and Vaishya classes. During this time, education was mostly centred in the family; brothers, sisters and cousins probably studied together under the family elders. Subsequently, when specialisation became the order of the day, students had to leave their homes and often to go to distant places to study under celebrated teachers. When there were competent lady teachers (acharyas) available, parents must have naturally preferred to send their daughters to study under them. But this number was not very large.

In technical subjects like theology, philosophy and medicine most of the experts were usually males, and advanced lady students used to go to them for their studies. But the number of lady students going for higher education was not large. Only higher education was confined to girls from cultured and well-to-do families.

Usually, ordinary girls who did not go in for higher education were educated in their own families by their fathers, uncles or brothers or by the local lady teachers.

On finishing her period of studentship, brahmacharya, a women was married to a learned young man. The celebrated seers of the archaic hymns and the highly renowned brahmavadinis of the Upanisads, Gargi and Maitreyio—for example—who displayed talent and temerity in participating in physical discussions, provide us with a measure of the intellectual attainments reached by women of the age. Down to the times of Apastamba, women appear to have pursued academic careers. As Apastamba notes that 'the knowledge which women possess is the completion of all study.' And later the author of *Amarkosa* has testified to this fact by interpreting acharya and upadhyaya as respectively 'one who herself in capable of expounding the hymns of the Vedas' and 'one who herself discourses on knowledge.' *Harita* coming still later has spoken both of women who are brahmavadinis and of those who are ordinary.

With the passage of time, the whole situation changed slowly. Women were denied education. In the *Manusmriti* we find restrictions that tended to deprive woman of her traditional status. The investiture of the sacred thread which initiated a person into the study of the Vedas came to be confined only to male children, the females being entitled to only one sacrament, namely marriage.

In the *Grhyasutra* sacraments, samskaras were allowed to be performed in the case of women also; but they were performed silently, i.e., without the Vedic Mantras. Women's education suffered a great deal on account of the new fashion of child marriage that had then began to come into vogue. By the beginning of the Christian era pre-puberty marriages become the order of the day.

Naturally, this meant a serious handicap to advanced

studies, which could not be obviously finished before the age of 12 or 13, which was the new marriageable age. Ultimately they had lost the status of the regenerate classes (dvijas); like the Sudras they were in course of time naturally regarded as unfit for reciting or even hearing Vedic prayers. By about the 8th or the 9th century A.D. the marriageable age of girls was further lowered to 9 or 10; this gave practically a death blow to any education worth the name.

It is pertinent to note that during the Muslim rule the percentage of literacy among Hindu women went further down with great rapidity. Rich and cultured families were as a rule ruined by the new political revolution; they were no longer in a position to make special arrangements for the education of their daughters. Some exceptional cases were found among the daughters of Rajput, Naır and Zamindar families, who could read and write. Society had a prejudice against female education; it was believed that a girl taught to read and write would become a widow. The only education which was thought to be necessary for them was to acquire the knowledge of the household duties. Their thoughts were mainly confined to such things which immediately concerned them, for example, food, clothings, ornaments, husbands, children, weddings, relations, neighbours, and so on.

Remarkably, girls belonging to the rich and well-to-do classes did receive some education in their respective homes without going to any 'Pathshala'. The courses of their study included Philosophy, Grammar, Mathematics, Drama, Music, Poetry and various other subjects relating to the Hindu 'Shastras' and the 'Puranas'. They received such an education that they frequently invited their opponents to challenge them in literary discussions, and by defeating them successfully, they established their scholarly reputation.

The illiteracy rate among the middle class Hindu women had reached its peak in the 19th century. Only after the advent of the British several steps were taken for the promotion of education among the girls. But the progress of female education was found to be very slow for several reasons 'Christian missionaries opened girls' schools (beginning in 1819), but high-caste Hindus would not allow their daughters to attend, as they feared attempts at conversion'.

It is significant to note that Ishvarchandra Vidyasagar foresaw that the future of women lay in their being educated, and he devoted himself to the propagation of female education. The Bethune School, founded in 1849, was the first institution in Calcutta for female education. A start was made in Bombay in the same year through the efforts of the boys of Elphinstone College, and in Ahmedabad, with one student, under the aegis of the Gujarat Vernacular Society.

Lord Dalhousie lent Government patronage to this movement. The rudimentary nature of female education in the 19th century India can be shown by literacy and educational statistics. In 1854, it was estimated that 7,000 girls (mostly native Christians) attended mission schools. While in 1882, there were approximately 1,27,000 female students less than 3 per cent of whom were above primary level. The literacy rates of both men and women were low, but the male literacy rate was 20 times the female literacy rate. In 1883, two Bengali Brahmo women became the first Indian Women college graduates; they attended Bethune College in Calcutta.

The number of women attending college rose very slowly. The early women college students were primarily Anglo, Indians Indian Christians, or Parsis. Report 1958-

59 and Report of the Education Commission 1964-66, Ministry of Education, Government of India, 1966, shows that by 1965-66, the number of girls in primary schools had risen to above 18 million and in secondary schools to 3.9 million.

The literacy rate was the lowest in areas with a high concentration of tribes and scheduled castes, who mostly worked as agricultural labourers. These women were not in a position to avail themselves of any of the educational or training facilities connected with the development process. When analysing the educational status of urban middle class women, it was found that there was a rapid expansion of women's education in the cities, above all in women's colleges and university education.

This was due to rise in the marriageable age of the girls. Economic conditions also helped its spread. Services of educated women were in great demand; these circumstances also helped the growth of female education.

Occupation

Now we will come to the field of occupation.

Remarkably, in the ancient period, the Aryans were mostly engaged in military or semi-military activities, as they were engaged in the task of subjugating the country. As there was no 'Purda' in the Aryan society women used to receive education of a fairly advanced type, therefore, their men could rely upon a great degree of cooperation from them. Women were engaged in agriculture, as well as in the manufacture of bows, arrows, and other war material. Female workers were also found in dying, embroidery and basket-making. Women in higher circles had also been found manufacturing bows and arrows, cloth and baskets in the Vedic period, but gave up these plebian professions in later times.

Women in the lower strata of society, however, continued to weave cloth, prepare baskets and participate in agriculture as before. During this time there were only two or three professions open to women in the higher sections of the society. The teaching career was very popular.

A women teacher was designated as 'Acharya'. Some of these lady teachers have been found to specialise even in abstruse and difficult branches of knowledge like theology and philosophy. Lady teachers teaching grammar, poetry and literature were very common. Medical career was also selected by some women. Among the works translated into Arabic in the 8th Century A.D. there was one on midwifery by a Hindu lady, whose name appears as Rusa in the Arabic grab. Lady doctors were found to be usually specialising in midwifery.

Further in the realm of business also we find that women suffered no disabilities. They do figure in the list of persons declared competent for entering into a valid contract. Women in lower classes and commercial and industrial circles used to take an active part in carrying on the business transactions of their families.

This position deteriorated slowly after the Muslim invasion. The prevalence of the 'Purdah' system during this period was only responsible for this deterioration, and had practically snatched the freedom of movement from out women and kept them confined within the four walls of their houses. They were also married at a very early age, so they could not find enough time and opportunity to carry on their studies. They were also not given any opportunity to enter the occupational fields.

After the advent of the British in India, there were great changes in the position of women. The first important step taken by the Britishers was encouragement of female education. 'Missionary schools were opened in many states of India. Followers of the Brahmo Samaj (a sect founded by Raja Ram Mohan Roy in 1828) and the Arya Samaj (founded by Swami Dayanand, a Kathiawar Brahmin, shortly after) who had, more or less, hived off from orthodox Hinduism, actively supported female education.' The popularity of female education was on an upward trend and year after year the number of girls attending schools increased. Apart from this general rise in female literacy, there were encouraging signs that Indian girls were prepared to go for higher education and even for careers. There also developed an economic incentive to higher education for girls among the middle classes.

The old antagonism to paid work for educated women was slowly dying, and girls who were able to get through the matriculation examination found respectable jobs waiting for them as teachers, clerks, typists and in many middle class families with no adult or able males, working girls fulfilled the role of breadwinners. As female education progressed, women began to take up careers too. In medicine, they found a profession particularly suited to their genius, and a regular 'Women's Medical Service' was organised and in many places in India women's hospitals were exclusively run by lady doctors. Took to law too, and some of the more energetic of them, even to engineering.

Woman, at present are trying to enter every type of profession. They now work in the Police force, as office secretaries, bus-conductors or shop assistants, and they can practise as doctors, lawyers or engineers; many are engaged in administrative and political services. The outlook of the Hindu woman has enlarged, her opinions find perspective, her creative energies are unfolded, her personality has developed; also she realises her rights and her place in society. Thus, we have found that in the modern times, women are trying to enter all kinds of professional fields. This supports the fact that women have got enough freedom now-a-days.

Freedom to Go out Alone

Once again in the ancient Vedic period the presence of ladies in social and public gatherings was a normal feature. The Vedic poets also describe gaily attired ladies going out for a function. It was found that women had sufficient liberty of going and walking about. They were not necessarily confined to the four-walls of their family house. Though the apartments in which they used to reside were secluded, ensuring privacy, yet they quite freely associated with others on occasions of festivals and rejoicings.

Notably, in the *Ramayana* and *Mahabharata*, it has been found that women and maidens decked with ornaments could fearlessly wander everywhere without male relatives to attend upon them. The Epic societies were mostly monarchical. This shows that the movements of women were in no way restricted. Women attended courts for business. They moved freely in public particularly on festive occasions or for witnessing any strange object or event. The ladies of royal families had their outdoor pleasures also. Subhadra was abducted when she was returning after attending the public festival at Raivataka.

The Kuru ladies went out to the forest for picnics and for visiting their relations. In Ramayana from some of the allusions it was found that women at the time took part in various types of recreations and other public activities. But inspite of this freedom, it was also found, particularly among the women of high class families, that they did not come out too frequently in front of the public. But slowly after this period, the freedom of women diminished. There were certain restrictions on their movements. They could go out of their house to visit their friends and relations, but they could not stay at their houses for the night.

They were to observe a certain amount of reserve in the presence of strangers. They were also not allowed to go out freely in the public or to attend any festivals. "Kautilya also records a state of society in which women had been denied liberty. According to him, a woman who goes out during day time, to sports or to see a woman or spectacles shall pay a fine of six panas."

The situation worsened with the advent of the Muslim rule. The adoption of the purdah and the lowering of the marriage age by the middle-class Hindus restricted the free movement of the women (the freedom of the women of Hindu royal families had been restricted earlier). At this time the two sexes operated in separate worlds which were mutually dependent. A women's sphere of activity was domesticated — she managed the home, prepared the food, and look care of the children. The man's sphere of activity was external — he provided for the family economically, and he participated in any other interactions with non-kin groups. With the lowering of the marriage age, inexperienced and uneducated wives became incapable of taking part in many activities outside their homes.

Naturally, husbands began to claim and exercise a greater control over them which proved harmful to their participation in the social and public life and activities. Husbands with narrow outlook would not allow their wives to mix freely with the outside world. Thus slowly the purdah system as well as the lowering of the marriage age of women started narrowing their sphere of activities. This position, however, continued till the beginning of the present century.

Many Indian women workers like Mrs. Anadibai Joshi, Pandita Ramabai and Mrs. Ramabai Ranade came forward and courageously proceeded with the work of female emancipation. Things however, changed when female education began to become more widely diffused. The sphere of women's activities have been found to be increasing since 1935.

Women have again started to come out of their houses and are being found participating in public life. They also have started taking part in every type of profession.

Purdah

Though having the sanction of tradition and religions, purdah is an evil system which has hampoered the progress of women. Recently in France and in one state of Canada purdah is banned.

Purdah literally means 'curtain'. But as a system, purdah means not only the Veil that covers Muslim women or the upper sari-end that Hindu women draw over their faces or their eyes, but purdah is also the symbol for a comprehensive system of rules, codes of conduct, folk-ways, the principle of which is the most radical form of sex segregation and seclusion of women. This seclusion can be achieved through walls, railings, curtains, veils, separate compartments in trains for men and women, separate seats in buses, through gestures like turning away of the head or looking down and also through silence.

Purdah means above all that a woman should never appear in public, and if that cannot be avoided, must protect herself from being looked at by men. The Purdah or the veil has not been found in the ancient Vedic period. At that time, we find girls often educated alongwith boys. There were even love-marriages taking place and many times both the boys and girls went together to see shows and sports. All this was not at all possible if Purdah system was observed in the society. The girls were not required to cover their heads even after marriage.

The Vedic marriage hymn requires the bride to be shown to all the assembled guests at the end of the marriage ritual. The hope was further expressed that the bride should be able to speak with composure in public assemblies down to her old age. Ladies were also found to go out to courts of law to establish their claims of inheritance.

There is no reference of any Purdah arrangement being made for their attendance. Nor does Rigveda 1, 167, 3 contain any reference to the Purdah system. In the Vedic age, we do find evidence of only a head-dress (ushnisha) worn by well-to-do family ladies. This head-dress was something like a pagree and not merely a piece of cloth for covering the head like the modern odhni. But this was also not very common, as the usual custom was to arrange the hair in different artistic plaits, which could not be revealed if the head was covered.

Slowly the head-dress also went out of fashion, and women started covering their heads by an odhni, or piece of cloth, which was used to cover their head and fall gracefully over their shoulders and back. Orthodox women found it more convenient to cover their head with a portion of their saries.

After this women started adopting the veil to cover their whole face. The earliest reference of Purdah has been found in the epics. In this period, Purdah was observed in certain royal families because it was thought that royal ladies should not come within the gaze of vulgar eyes. It was also adopted as a sign of prestige. But some other examples have also been found in the epics, which go against the prevalence of Purdah. It has been found that when Kausalya, Kaikeyi and Sumitra went to Chitrakuta to induce Rama to return to Ayodhya, they moved about in public without any veil. Sita herself feels no embarrassment when she is moving through the streets of Ayodhya. In the forests too, which were infested with demons and enemies, she moves about without any veil. Draupadi's public appearance in the gambling hall presupposes an entire absence of the Purdah. Neither Kunti nor Gandhari are seen to be observing it. But together with this it has been said that their is no objection if women come out in public on occasions of marriages, svayamvaras, sacrifices and public calamities. This clearly shows that except for these occasions, she should remain in Purdah in normal life.

However, it was found, found that soon after the beginning of the Christian era, a section of society began to advocate a greater seclusion of women. This was particularly found among the royal families, who thought it desirable that their ladies should be seen only by a select few; when moving in public they should put on a veil.

Thus, the covering of the face with veil, was started in the Hindu Society. During that period we still do not find any trace of Purdah being observed within the family. It was always seen that the daughter-in-law had to pay her respects to elderly relations by bowing at their feet. We do not find anywhere that the father-in-law or the elder brother-in-law could not see the face of a daughter-in-law as we find now-a-days in northern India. The adoption of Purdah by the ruling and aristocratic families of Hindu community increased just after the advent of the Muslim rule.

This was accepted by the Hindu society partly in imitation of the manners of the conquerors, and partly as an additional protection for the women folk. In the Muslim ruling families the Purdah was so strict that a message had to be passed through three intermediaries before it could reach the desired person in the 'Zenana.'

The Hindu chiefs and nobles also followed the examples of their overlords. At this time, the seclusion of women had become very rigid, not only among the higher classes, but also among the lower middle classes, who could move out-of-doors only with a veil over their faces. The Hindu women in this period were illiterate and inexperienced. The times were unsettled, there was a general feeling of insecurity and Hindu life and honour did not count for much in the eyes of the conquerors.

The Purdah gave them additional protection while out on a journey, and so it was welcomed by Hindu women as well. By the 15th and the 16th centuries, the Purdah system had become quite common among the rich Hindu families of Bengal and the United Provinces. In Rajputana the custom became universal in the ruling families. This was regarded as an essential sign of respectability. Women of the peasant and working classes could not afford to remain in seclusion as they had to move out for their daily work. They would slightly cover their face with the end of their saris when a stranger passed by. The seclusion of women continued till the British period. In the British period, there was political struggle in India for bringing Indian women out of their age-old seclusion. Education and the prohibition of child marriage also had worked against the veil.

The political awakening among the women also had done much to weaken the forces of Purdah. The salient features of the non-cooperation movement was that a large number of women left the seclusion of their homes to fight side by side with their men. In the modern times, Purdah is diminishing. Social reformers and medical practitioners have started pointing towards its evil consequences. The education, which women have now begun to receive in large numbers, is proving fatal to the custom. Thus now-a-days, we find that people have started realising that this custom is not at all beneficial for the present society. It is only education which has helped in changing the traditional views and attitudes.

Dress Codes

The Vedic literature does not give enough information about the dress of the women of that age. The vocabulary itself of this period has got no separate words to denote women's clothes. Same words are used to denote the different clothes worn by both men and women. An under-garment (vasah antaram) and an upper garment (paridhanam) were generally used by both the sexes. A waist band was used round the lower garment. Both the garments were coloured in case of women. There is no information or clue as to how the lower garment or sari was worn in the Vedic days. The art of weaving was well-developed and it is quite certain that the sari was a long piece, about five or six yards in length.

Thus we find that in the Vedic days women were usually wearing saris, as it is worn in the modern times. The epics also show that the women usually preferred to wear a sari. At home, only one sari was worn, which used to cover the shoulders, and bosom as well. An additional upper garment or shawl was sometimes used as a ceremonial dress. Jackets, blouses and frocks seem to have come into practice in the plains of northern India, when they were included in the dominions of the Scythians, the Kushanas and other Central Asiatic Invaders.

As these conquerors came from a very cold region, they were accustomed to wear shirts, trousers and overcoats. In the Mathura and Gandhara sculptures, which belong to the period of Kushana supremacy (c. 50.A.D. to c. 300 A.D.) women being to appear in blouses and frocks. In one bas-relief at Mathura even Sapta Matrikas are seen wearing frocks. During this period, people had a general prejudice against stitched clothes, and women were for a long time reluctant to wear jackets, blouses and frocks. Only dancing girls were adopting the new fashion in dress. So it is quite clear that only women of this class and not of rank were seen wearing jackets and blouses.

At Ajanta, only maid-servants are found wearing shirts and jackets; ladies of position were avoiding them. Slowly stitching was introduced in the bodice, but the prejudice against full-fledged jackets, blouses and frocks did not decrease. These became common only among a section of ladies in the Muslim period.

After the establishment of the Mahomaden rule, the lahanga became very popular among women of higher society, especially in Rajputana and northern India. This lahanga was quite unknown for a long time. In some Mathura sculptures of the 2nd century A.D. only maid-servants or milkwomen are seen using it. It only became common after century of Muslim rule. In South India since the Muslim influence was less felt, even grown up women did not take to the lahanga. From the Moghul period paintings, it is quite clear that Hindu women under the influence of the Muslim rule had started wearing a lahanga or a pyjama. They used to wear a lahanga or pyjama down from their waist. The former was sewn in different artistic designs, and nothing was usually worn over it. The pyjama was a simple one and usually a short sari was worn over it. The bust was covered with a bodice or a jacket. An upper garment or odhni was also in fashion, which hung from the head covering a portion of the back. In this period, the women of Bengal usually wore saris. The quality and delicacy of the saris varied according to the status and economic condition of the wearer.

The women of richer and higher classes generally wore saris made of famous Muslim and other fine silk and cotton fabrics. The women of lower and poorer sections of the society wore a coarse sari known as Khuiya. In Orissa, poor women mostly covered the lower parts of their bodies with leaves.

Women did not change themselves even in the British rule. They continued to use their old dress consisting of sari, a bodice and a shawl. In the modern times, shirts and frocks have become common only among urban girls. But ladies still prefer to wear a sari. The dress of the average Hindu women, however, still continues to be the old traditional one of the province.

After going through the main aspects of women's liberation, we can say that women's position differed from culture to culture and from time to time, more liberal in some and too exploitative in others. In the Vedic period, the society had definitely given liberty to women in every field. But slowly from the Smriti period onwards their exploitation started, which continued till the British period.

The Britishers introduced a new system of education in society. This proved helpful in awakening our suppressed

Indian women. It was then that the Indian women started opposing the exploitative nature of men and began to work towards a new concept of humanism. Thus there emerged an Indian Women's Movement roughly from 1880. Women's movement participants were drawn from the tiny sector of urban educated families. Members from all major religious communities were represented in the Indian Women's Movement although high-caste Hindus appear to have been numerically dominant.

It is pertinent to note that were two different conceptions of improving the position of women in the ideology of the Indian Women's Movement. In the first, the goal was women's upliftment. The meaning attached to 'women's upliftment' was reform in the social practices so as to enable women to play a more important and more constructive role in society. In the second conception, the goal was equal rights for men and women. The meaning attached to 'equal rights' was the extension of the civil rights enjoyed by men in the political, economic and familial spheres to women. The potential of women in development, according to the women's upliftment conception involved expanding and strengthening female roles in society. Female roles-mother, wife, home-maker, and female values-sacrifice, loyalty, non-violence, were presented as relevant to the problems of development. In fact, the women's upliftment argument was that women's role in development rested on her female roles and qualities.

Women's Movement leaders argued that debilitating social practices should be changed and women should be educated so that they may perform their roles in a more enlightened manner, and female values may have a more widespread impact on society. The activities suggested by the women's upliftment conception were primarily educational and social in nature although legislation to abolish certain practices which restricted women's potential was also implied. Women workers like Mrs. Anandibai Joshi, Pandita Ramabai and Mrs. Ramabai Ranade came forward to work for women's emancipation. They were mainly concerned with the problems of female education, maternity welfare, widow remarriage, the abolition of Purdah custom, etc.

Not only in India, but also in other countries, the women's Liberation Movement had started even where women had enough freedom. There the freedom was associated with sex and licence. It was found that well educated women inspite of their contribution to management, commerce, industry, and other activities where men still have a full monopoly, are too frustrated because of their secondary role and because of their being chained as a housewife.

The Women's Liberation Movement was also started in the United States. Betty Friedan, author of the book 'The Feminine Mystique' started a civil rights organisation after 1967 called NOW (National Organisation of Women). NOW members agitated for the Equal Rights Amendment Bill, to ban sex discrimination in jobs, start Day Dare Centres, and get tax deductions for working mothers, maternity leave rights, social security benefits, and the right of a woman to control her own reproductive role. This was a purely middle class movement. In 1974, the New York Radical Feminists Conference Discussed with brutal Frankness the matter of motherhood. Radical women emphasise that motherhood is too big a responsibility not to be shared by husbands. They feel that women must have the freedom not to have children.

In traditional Indian society, a woman is not particularly important, but a mother is all important. The notions that dominate women in the West about freedom from male and other oppressions, the need for privacy, for self-realisation are not of primary importance to women in other parts of the world. Indian women are concerned mainly with liberating themselves from the male dominating society, where they are unable to receive high education, to go out of their houses whenever they please, marry whenever they feel like and so on. There are also many other aspects of liberation in out study towards which the attitude of our respondents has to be found out. Some of these aspects do tell us about the homely comforts which are essential for a woman to save her energy and time from her house job and then participate in other activities of the society. If we want a woman to contribute something to society, then we should first liberate her from the four-walls of her home by giving her some comforts.

When the woman was uneducated, when she had no political, social or economic rights at that time she was found to be totally dependent on man. But let us see as to how much she feels that she should depend on a man after getting education and becoming economically independent.

In Western countries, sex education for children in schools and colleges is becoming quite popular. In India importance is not given to such an education.

It is also worthwhile analysing the attitude of the working women towards pre-marital sex relations. When we tried to see the attitude of our respondents towards dominating family members, it was found that 14 per cent married women did not mind their family members dominating, while 79 per cent were against it.

REFERENCES

A.S. Altekar, *The Position of Women in Hindu Civilisation,* Motilal Banarasidass, Delhi, 1978, p.15.

B.N. Ganguli, *Emma Goldman, Portrait of a Rebel Women,* Allied Publishers Pvt. Ltd., New Delhi, 1979, p. 43.

Baboo Ishuree Dass, *Domestic Manners and Customs of the Hindoos of North India,* Medical Hall Press, Banaras, 1960, p. 155.

Devaki Jain (ed.), *Indian Women,* Publications Division, Ministry of Information and Broadcasting Government of India, New Delhi, 1975, p. xiv.

Jogesh C. Bagal, 'Women's Education in Eastern India (calcutta, 1956). p. 62, (c.f.) Jana Matson Everett, *Women and Social Change in India,* Heritage Publishers, New Delhi, 1979, p.31.

K.M. Kapadia, *Marriage and Family in India,* Oxford University Press, Calcutta, 1972, p. 252.

Lakshi Misra, 'Education of Women in India: 1921-1966' (Bombay, 1966), pp. 33-34.

Maria Mies, *Indian Women and Patriarchy,* Concept Publishing Company, New Delhi, 1980, p. 131.

P. Thomas, *Indian Woman Through the Ages,* Asia Publishing House, Bombay, 1964. p. 311.

Shakuntala Jayal, *The Status of Women in the Epics,* Motilal Banarasidass, Patna, 1966, p. 38.

Tara Ali Baig, *India's Woman Power,* S. Chand & Co. Pvt. Ltd., New Delhi, 1976, p. 45.

11

The SAARC Decade Plan of Action for the Girl Child (1991-2000)

> "The weaker sex is stronger because of the weakness of stronger sex for the weaker sex."

In fact developing Asian more particularly South Asian countries are most populous. They constitute the major section of world population despite of scanty geographical area with them. It properly developed womenpower can prove a boon for them. SAARC is an organization of some South Asian countries.

Here in this chapter we will reproduce the text of SAARC Decade Plan of Action for the Girl Child (1991-2000).

PART I : GUIDING PRINCIPLES

1.1 The improvement in the status of the girl child is indicated by the annual statistics. The gap between the sexes has narrowed down in infant Mortality Rate, from 98 for girls and 96 for males in 1985 to 80 for females and 79 for males in 1992, in age-specific mortality rates and in the improved enrolment rate of girls over the years. 115.3% for boys and 86.0% for girls in 1990-91 to 115.3% for boys and 92.9% for girls in 1993-94. Adolescent girls scheme, State schemes for Girl Child, DPEP, National Nutrition Policy, National Creche Fund, Indira Mahila Yojana and the rise in singulate mean age at marriage to 19.20 in the year 1984 from 18.90 years in 1981 for females.

1.2 The National Plan of Action for the Girl Child (copy enclosed) has clearly spelt out the goals and strategies for girls related to survival, health, education, training, protection against exploitation and abuse.

1.3 During the period under review several programmes and communication efforts were planned and executed to bring about change in the social attitudes and behavioural practices towards the girl child these include launching of the adolescent Girls Scheme, District Primary Education Programmes. Awareness Generation Programmes, Gender Sensitisation Programmes for officials of the Government and functionaries of the Non-Governmental Organisations (NGOs), para-legal training programmes, media campaigns on the girl-child in several parts of the country and production and telecast of audio-visual spots and films on girl child on the National television network of the country, children's Enrichment Experiment through Radio (CHEER) Project etc.

1.4 The implementation of the SAARC Decade Plan of Action for the girl child is good. However, monitoring has to be improved by collecting sex disaggregated data.

1.5 The major constraints faced during the period in implementing the SAARC Decade Plan of Action include the socio-cultural bias, prevailing social attitude, paucity of genderwise segregated data in various sectors resource constraint etc.

PART II : DECADE GOALS AND PRIORITY CONCERNS HEALTH AND NUTRITION

2.1 Latest Data

(a) Infant Mortality Rate (IMR) for girls declined from 94 per thousand in 1988 to 73 per thousand 1994. The under 5 mortality rate for girl children declined from 39 per thousand in 1988 to 27.2 per thousand in 1991.

(b) The National Evaluation of ICDS — A National Survey conducted in 1992 shows that 21.85% children were moderately malnourished and 5.4% were severely malnourished in ICDS blocks and in non ICDS blocks 24.2% children were moderately malnourished and 7.0% were severely malnourished (Moderate-between 60% to 75% of standard weight) severe — 60% or below of standard weight.

Action

(a and b) The Govt. of India has identified 180 focal districts in the country with reference to vital indices and literacy related data for specialised intervention through innovative programmes. The ICDS programme has been sanctioned to cover all 5291 community development blocks and 310 urban slums in 1995-96 and will help to reduce infant and child mortality and malnutrition. Special intervention programmes include schemes such as those in Tamil Nadu, Haryana (Apni Beti Apana Dhan) launched in 1991, Punjab and Andhra Pradesh to improve the status of the Girl Child. The National Policy for Empowerment of Women drafted recently, has elimination of discrimination and violation of the rights of the Girl Child as a major component. The scheme for Adolescent Girls has been launched in 507 blocks in the country on experimental basis to fight malnutrition (including stunting) and lack of preparedness for adult roles as women.

2.2 Latest Data and Action

(a) The Department of Education has introduced various programmes to achieve the goals of universalisation of elementary education. The Plan of Action follows a decentralised approach with district specific plans within the framework of micro-planning. The programmes in operation are Operation Blackboard, Minimum levels of learning, Scheme of Operationalising Micro-planning and Scheme of Non-formal Education. These programmes aiın at bringing about substantial improvement in the facilities and quality of education in primary schools, along with improvement in the existing level of learning achievement of children. Under the scheme of Operation Blackboard, 91 per cent of the primary schools had been covered till 1992-93. Under Minimum levels of learning, about 15 NGOs have have been identified and sanctioned projects to implement the programme covering 2,000 primary schools. A major initiative of the Education Department has been the District Primary Education Programme (DPEP) launched in November, 1994 which lays emphasis on micro-planning, involvement of communities and gender focus. The programme is implemented in a mission mode through partnership between the centre, the State Government and the Village Education Committee for the holistic development of primary education. Initiated in 42 districts in seven states, the DPEP is being expanded to cover all the major States and will be in operation in 110 districts by 1997.

(b) To enhance female literacy under the Non-formal education (NFE) Programme for children in the age-group 6-14 years, 76 million were enrolled and out of these 47 million were made literate upto the year 1994. The number of exclusively girl centres have been increased to 99,252 which accounts for 44% of the total centres. To increase access of girls under 16 years to opportunities for basic education beyond formal school system, coeducation centres and those exclusively for girls are funded by the Government under the NFE Programme. Besides this, District Primary Education Programme (DPEP), total literacy campaigns (TLCs) and Mahila Samakhya are the initiatives for facilitating universalisation access of girls to basic education opportunities. Lok Jumbish in Rajasthan and Bihar Education Project in Bihar are regional innovative interventions for universalisation of education opportunities.

(c) The equity ratio in enrolment of girls at primary and upper primary stages has improved from 83.3 in 1990-91 to 86.7 in 1994-95. The All India Educational Survey (1993) reported improvement in primary schools gross enrolment ratio by 42% overall and 7.5% amongst girls over a period of 7 years from 1986 to 1993. In rural areas, 36 million more girls (in the age-group of 5-14 years) are now going to primary schools. DPEP has been taken up in 42 districts of 7 states having low levels of female literacy and the programme has specific interventions for girl like alternative schooling, flexible school timings, gender sensitive curricula and recruitment of women teachers.

(d) The NFE centres exclusively for girls have been increased from 25% to 44% and have a Central government assistance of 90% of the operational cost. To promote female literacy, it has been decided that at least 50% of teachers under Operation Black board should be women. The participation of women and adolescents in the TLCs has risen to 62%, 113 more Non-Governmental Organisations (NGOs) have been sanctioned about 8,000 additional centres under NFE programme during 1995-96.

Marriage and Motherhood

2.3 (a) The minimum age of marriage of women has been raised to 18 years. In the age-group of 15-19 years 30.1% women were married and in the age-group of 20-24 years, 74.8% women were married, as per data available for 1992. The mean age at "effective marriage" for females was 19.5 years in 1992, as compared to 18.3 years in 1981. The government has initiated several programmes for education, vocational training and employment of girls and young women to make them self-reliant and gainfully employed; in order to facilitate reduction in proportion of early marriages of adolescent girls and young women.

(b) The age-specific fertility rates (ASFR) have declined for women in all age-groups between 1981 and 1991. For females in age-group 15-19 years the ASFR has declined from 88.3 in 1987 to 74.4 in 1992. The government has stepped up its efforts to reach families in terms of access to and promotion of usage of contraceptives for delaying first pregnancy, through the existing health care machinery and NGOs as well. A project to strengthen IEC activities for dissemination of information on sexuality and reproductive health of women and adolescents is under consideration of the Government. The village level women's groups called "Mahila Swasthya Sanghas" are being organised rapidly for the purpose.

2.4 About 89.3% of the rehabilitations have at least one safe source of drinking water. There are less than 1000 villages throughout the whole country without a safe source of drinking water. No case of guineaworm infestation has been reported in 31 States/UTs. Rajasthan the only state which is still not free from guineaworm. Pilot projects for fluorosis control have been started in 5 States of Andhra Pradesh, Haryana, Rajasthan, Punjab and Gujarat, where incidence of fluorosis had been reported. Training has been given to women in some areas to enable them to play an active role in using and repairing handpumps for the supply of drinking water and were associated with selection of sites for hand pump and other water sources. A study of 69 such cases indicated positive results.

In the area of sanitation, the surveys conducted so far have not effectively captured the inputs and achievements of private investments in the sector. According to available estimates about 46.63% of the urban population and 11% of the rural population has been provided with sanitation facilities so far. For women some exclusive sanitary facilities have been provided in selected rural areas, by way of village sanitation complexes for women.

2.5 The girl child workers are estimated to number

around 7.6 million as per the 43rd National Sample Survey, 1987-88. There are no reliable estimates of girl children engaged in prostitution. Girl Child workers are mostly in the unorganised sector or in domestic work, but no specific figures are available regarding their number within these sectors.

2.6 India has constitutional and legal provisions for protection, development and welfare of children. The National Policy for children and the National Plan of Action for the Girl Child provide the framework for interventions to improve the status of the girl child. The member state has set up the National Authority for Elimination of Child and Labour and a Central Advisory Committee and State Level Advisory Committees for eradication of child prostitution. A scheme for street children nas also been launched to enable protection and development of street children.

Voluntary agencies are provided assistance to enable children of prostitutes to be removed from the exploitative social environment and to protect and develop them.

The State Government of Madhya Pradesh has launched a Scheme called Jabali for protecting girl children from being induced not prostitution, for providing residential education, vocational skills training, assistance for asset acquisition and increasing awareness about the evils of prostitution.

PART III : POLICY SUPPORT

3.1 The gender specific goals for decade of the girl Child in India are :—

- Survival and protection of the girl child and safe motherhood which will touch upon various aspects of health, nutrition, immunisation, maternity and child health, referral facilities, safe drinking water and sanitation;

- Overall development of the girl child with the ultimate objectives of freeing her from the stereotypical roles and the shackles of prejudices, making her economically independent and self reliant thus facilitating her mainstreaming into national development with an equal status and;
- Special protection for vulnerable girl children in difficult circumstances and belonging to special groups who are economically and socially deprived or disabled, physically or mentally.

3.2 Besides National Plan of Action for the SAARC Decade of the Girl Child, recently Government of India has drafted a National Policy for the Empowerment of women. The policy would among other things lay down strategies and action points to bridge the gap between the constitutional and legal equality. It would continuously guide and inform action at every level and in every sector by mainstreaming gender perspectives into all laws, regulations, plans, policies and programmes and budgetary allocations.

3.3 The action plan goals for girl child have been incorporated in Five-Year Plan of the country. Development of Women and Child Development identified specific thrust areas relating to each of the departments including Ministry of Health and Family Welfare, Rural Development, Education, Urban Development, Welfare, Labour for covergence of the services. These thrust areas were communicated to all concerned for taking necessary action towards integration/convergence of services.

3.4 In order to eradicate child prostitution Government of India has taken many steps. In a public interest litigation, the Supreme Court of India passed an order after hearing various parties on the subject "Child Prostitution" which stated that the Central and State government should set up Advisory Committees to make suggestions for the measure to be taken to eradicate child prostitution. In accordance with this Govt. of India constituted a Central Advisory Committee under the Chairpersonship of Secretary, Deptt. of Women and Child Development. The Central Advisory Committee has studied the problem of child prostitution and submitted its report and recommendations to eradicate child prostitution. The implementation of the recommendations by various Ministries and State Governments is being monitored by the Central State Advisory Committees.

3.5 Deptt. of Women and Child Development has set up an Inter-Ministerial Coordination Committee to monitor the implementation of the Action Plan on girl child. Besides Women's Bureau in the Deptt. also monitors the various programmes relating to women including girl children.

3.6 The information are taken care under the points 5.4, 5.5 and 5.7

PART IV : ADVOCACY AIMS

4.1 The Women's Development Division of the Nation Institution of Public Cooperation and Child Development, New Delhi organises training programmes with a focus on gender issues. These training programmes were organised at national, regional and state levels.

Some of important programmes include — para legal training, training of elected women representative of Panchayats; Leadership and Organisation, training of voluntary agencies reaching women, awareness and gender sensitisation programmes, incorporation of gender issues in development programmes etc. The participants of these programmes included government officials, representatives of voluntary agencies, academic and technical insitutions.

4.2 Government attaches great importance to those efforts which trigger changes in social attitudes towards girl child. An integrated media campaign projecting positive image of both women and girl child through electronic media, print and film media is the most important component of Government strategy. A large number of TV spots, quickies, messages on closed circuit TV systems in railway stations, documentary films, radio programmes with positive messages about the girl child and women were produced and disseminated by the Deptt. of Women and Child Development. The mass mobilisation activities, training curricula, literacy primers and post literacy activities under the Total Literacy Campaigns give primacy to messages of girl child equality and development.

4.3 Many of the programmes initiated by government and Voluntary agencies are on-going programmes. Many awareness camps/seminars/conferences/workshop had been organised by Government, academic and technical institutions, National Commission on Women, Bilateral and Multilateral organisations on various issues relating to girl child e.g. removing bias in health, education, nutrition, breast feeding, immunisation on violence against girl child, etc.

4.4 Department of Education along with National Council for Education, Research and Training (NCERT) have taken corrective steps to remove gender bias in school text books. National Literacy Mission has incorporated Girl Child and women's issues in their literacy primers, and post literacy books.

4.5 Integrated Child Development Services (ICDS) with its opportunities for early childhood development seeks to reduce both socio-economic and gender inequalities. In order to better address concerns for girl child, it was found necessary to design intervention for adolescent girls seeking to break the inter-generational life-cycle of nutritional disadvantage and providing a supportive environment for self development. For the first time in the country a special intervention was designed for adolescent girls, using the ICDS infrastructure. This intervention focusses on school drop-out girls in the age-group 11-18 years to meet their needs of self development, nutrition and health, education, literacy, recreation and skills format.

4.6 The Programme Evaluation Organisation of Planning Commission the Research Division of the Deptt. of Women and Child Development, National Institute of Public Cooperation and Child Development, National Institute of Nutrition, National Council of Educational Research and Training have conducted research studies about situation, impact of schemes on children including girl child, their health, nutrition and psychological development. Besides many micro-level studies have been conducted by Home Science Colleges, Women Studies Centres and other research institutions.

PART V : STRATEGIC DIRECTIONS

5.1 The 73rd and the 74th constitutional amendments have created vibrant and new partnerships to reach the most disadvantaged, deserving and the most vulnerable young children.

5.2 With the recently launched Indira Mahila Yojana (IMY), new possibilities are unfolding for ICDS to promote process for women's empowerment. The Indira Mahila Yojana has three components-convergence of inter-sectoral services; awareness creation; and income generation activities. It has been initiated in 200 ICDS blocks during the year.

5.3 Many Departments in Central Ministries and Central Social Welfare Board have started schemes for voluntary agencies. The 73rd constitutional amendment provides ample opportunities to women in governance at local level. Panchayati Raj institutions have been allotted many subjects including women and child development.

5.4 Greater and effective involvement of NGOs has been attempted to promote the interest of girl child. Media Campaigns have been organised by voluntary agencies to remove gender bias. Recently Panchayati Raj Institutions have also been involved. Efforts have been made to sensitise the women elected representatives of Panchayati Raj Institutions. A number of schemes of the Department and other Ministries/Departments are implemented through NGOs. Many NGOs are also implementing the ICDs projects. Department of Women and Child Development has set up a NGO cell system of networking with NGO with UNICEF support.

5.5 The Department of Women and Child Development has the overall responsibility of monitoring using its extensive network for gathering community level information on programme implementation. A Monitoring Cell established at the Deptt. collects and analyses periodic data, reports. A National level ICDS Management Information System (MIS) working group now collects gender disaggregated information. Each state also has MIS Coordination Cell. It collects information through Monitoring proforma in which data on boys and girls are recorded. Efforts are being made for the development of Women's Information Network System (WINS) in collaboration with the National Informatics Centre

(NIC) as a part of their country wide NICNET and DISNIC Network.

5.6 Inter Ministerial Coordination Committees have been set up for strict monitoring of the implementation of National Plan of Action for the SAARC decade of the Girl Child. The Committee has stressed upon modifying proforma etc. to collect disaggregated data by the concerned Departments/Ministries and furnishing the same to the committee.

5.7 Government has revised its many monitoring performance by including gender disaggregated data. All efforts are made to collect information on girl child at various levels by different departments.

5.8 National Institute of Public Cooperation and Child Development (NIPCCD) along with other National level and State level institutes organise training programmes on various issues relating to gender and girl child. Department of Personnel and Training of Govt. of India along with other administrative institutes impart training on gender issues.

5.9 The training institutions, home science colleges, schools of social work women studies centres organised workshops, seminars, awareness camps and conducted research studies relating to girl child.

PART VI : RESOURCE MOBILISATION

6.1 The overall allocation of funds at the national level for the Department of Women and Child which covers various concerns of Girl Child has gone up over the years from Rs. 3510 million in 1990-91 to Rs. 8950 million in 1996-97. In addition State Governments urban and local bodies also have substantially increased their allocation for the development of women and children in this decade. A multi-centre study on Declining Sex Ratio and another one on Girl Child and the Family have been funded by the Department of Women and Child Development from its research related resource allocation during the period. There is a provision of Rs. 25 lakh for research, monitoring, evaluation and implementation of innovative action-cum-research projects.

6.2 Private and public sector participation in various development programmes is also encouraged by tax incentives and advocacy support the Decade Plan of Action.

6.3 External aid has been provided for programmes and projects related to the girl child and Young Women by DANIDA, UNICEF, UNIFEM, World Bank, NORAD, IFAD, SIDA, CARE, WFP etc.

Appendix

APENDIX - A
TOWARDS EQUALITY: REPORT OF THE COMMITTEE ON THE STATUS OF WOMEN IN INDIA

December 1974. Government of India, Ministry of Education and Social Welfare, Department of Social Welfare, New Delhi

The Committee on the Status of Women in India (CSWI) was appointed by the Government of India in 1971 (i) to evaluate the changes that had taken place in the status of women as a result of the constitutional, legal and administrative measures adopted since independence, (ii) to examine the impact of the complex processes of social change on various sections of Indian women, and (iii) to suggest measures which would enable women to play their full and proper role in building up the nation.

The Committee set up six Task Forces and two Study Groups to examine the changes in the field of social life, law, economic, participation, educational development, political status, and women's welfare and development. The summary of recommendations of the CSWI was as follows:

SUMMARY OF RECOMMENDATIONS

CHAPTER III—THE SOCIO-CULTURAL SETTING OF WOMEN'S STATUS

The review of the disabilities and constraints on women,

which stem from socio-cultural institutions, indicates that the majority of women are still very far from enjoying the rights and opportunities guaranteed to them by the Constitution. Society has not yet succeeded in framing the required norms or institutions to enable women to fulfil the multiple roles that they are expected to play in India today. On the other hand, the increasing incidence of practices like dowry indicate a further lowering of the status of women. They also indicate a process of regression from some of the norms developed during the Freedom Movement. We have been perturbed by the finding of the content analysis of periodicals in the regional languages, that concern for women and their problems, which received an impetus during the Freedom Movement, has suffered a decline in the last two decades. The social laws, that sought to mitigate the problems of women in their family life, have remained unknown to a large mass of women in this country who are as ignorant of their legal rights today as they were before independence (3.362).

1. We realise that changes in social attitudes and institutions cannot be brought about very rapidly. It is, however, necessary to accelerate this process of change by deliberate and planned efforts. Responsibility for this acceleration has to be shared by the State and the community, particularly that section of the community which believes in the equality of women. We, therefore, urge that community organisations, particularly women's organisations should mobilise public opinion and strengthen social efforts against oppressive institutions like polygamy, dowry, ostentatious expenditure on wedding and child marriage, and mount a campaign for the dissemination of information about the legal rights of women to increase their awareness. This is a joint responsibility which has to be shared by community organisations, legislators who have helped to

frame these laws and the Government which is responsible for implementing them (3.36).

CHAPTER IV—WOMEN AND THE LAW

2. Eradication of Polygamy in Muslim Law

Full equality of sexes can hardly be possible in a legal system which permits polygamy and a social system which tolerates it (4.13). The only personal law, which has remained impervious to the changing trend from polygamy to monogamy is Muslim Law (4.14).

The solution of standard contracts fails to provide a substantive relief to the first wife with children. As the second marriage is not invalidated, the position of the husband is not prejudicially affected but for the financial implications arising out of the step. The deterrance of the criminal sanction when a person intends to contract a second marriage is absent. Further, it is ineffective in cases of fake conversions to Islam from other religions, to circumvent the prohibition against bigamy. The remedy is out of step with the position in the other personal laws in India and should be rejected (4.20).

While the desirability of reform in Muslim Law is generally acknowledged, the Government has taken no steps towards changing the law for over two decades on the view that public opinion in the Muslim community did not favour a change. This view cannot be reconciled with the declaration of equality and social justice. We are of the opinion that ignoring the interest of Muslim women is a denial of social justice. The right of equality, like the right of free speech, is an individual right (4.26).

2. We are of the firm view that there can be no compromise on the basic policy of monogamy being the rule for all

communities in India. Any compromise in this regard will only perpetuate the existing inequalities in the status of women (4.30).

3. Enforcement of Provision Against Bigamy under Hindu Marriage Act

(a) In our opinion the right to initiate prosecution for bigamy should be extended to persons other than girl's family with prior permission of the Court to prevent the current wide-spread violation of a most salutary provision of the law which very clearly lays down the social policy of the country (4.33.34).

(b) We recommended that the words 'solemnised' should be replaced by the words "goes through a form of marriage". Further an explanation should be added to section 17 of the Hindu Marriage Act that an omission to perform some of the essential ceremonies by parties shall not be constructed to mean that the offence of bigamy was not committed, if such a ceremony of marriage gives rise to a de facto relationship of husband and wife (4.39).

(c) We recommended that a provision be introduced in Section 6 of the Hindu Marriage Act to the effect that nothing contained in the Hindu Marriage Act shall prevent a court from granting an injunction against a proposed bigamous marriage under the Act or under the provisions of the specific Relief Act, 1963.

4. Reform of Marriage Laws Prevalent in Former French and Portuguese Territories

In our opinion continuation of such diverse laws (permitting polygamy), contradictory to our social policy, in these territories is totally unjustified. We recommend the immediate replacement of these laws by the Hindu Marriage Act 1965 (4.51).

5. Restraint of Child Marriages

(a) When the legal age of marriage in case of a female is below the age of discretion she cannot be expected to form an intelligent opinion about her partner in life. The policy of law which permits the marriage of a girl's before she is physically and mentally mature is open to serious question. Child marriage is one of the significant factors leading to the high incidence of suicide among young married women in India. Therefore, increasing the marriage age of girls to eighteen years is desirable (4.61).

(b) An anchronism in Muslim Law governs some sects. After puberty, a Muslim male in all sects and a Muslim female belonging to the Hanafi and Ithana Ashari sects can marry without a guardian. 'But a Malik, Shafi or Daudhi or Sulayamani Bohra virgin cannot marry without a guardian and her only remedy is to change over to the Hanafi School and marry according to its tenets (4.62).

In our opinion a change in the law to remove the existing disability in these sub-schools, to bring them in conformity with the Hanafi law is necessary (4.63).

(c) There are large scale violations of the Child Marriage Restraint Act, particularly in the rural areas. The State of Gujarat has made it a cognisable offence with provisions for appointment of a Child Marriage Prevention Officer.

We recommend that all offences under the Child Marriage Restraint Act should be made cognisable, and special officers appointed to enforce the law (4.65).

(d) The right to repudiate a child marriage by a girl on attaining majority is provided under Muslin Law if the following facts are established:

(i) that she was given in marriage by her father or other guardian before she attained the age of 15;

(ii) that the repudiated the marriage before she attained the age of 18;

(iii) that the marriage was not consummated (4.67).

In our view the right to repudiate the marriage on attaining majority should be made available to girls in all communities whether the marriages was consummated or not (4.68).

(e) The Parsee Marriage and Divorce Act provides that "no suit shall be brought in any court to enforce any marriage between Parsees or any contract connected with or arising out of any such marriage, if, at the date of the institution of the suit the husband shall not have completed the age of 16 years or the wife shall not have completed the age of 14 years."

We recommend legislation prohibiting courts from granting any relief in respect of a marriage solemnised in violation of the age requirements prescribed by law, unless both the parties have completed the age of 18 years (4.69).

6. Registration of Marriages

Compulsory registration of marriages as recommended by the U.N. will be an effective check on child and bigamous marriages, offer reliable proof of marriages and ensure legitimacy and inheritence rights of children (4.70-4.72).

We recommend that registration should be made compulsory for all marriages (4.73).

7. Prevention of Dowry

The Dowry Prohibition Act 1961 has signally failed to

achieve its purpose. In spite of the persistent growth of this practice there are practically no cases reported under the Act (4.75). There is hardly any evidence of social conscience in this regard in the country today (4.77). The educated youth is grossly indifferent to the evil and unashamedly contributed to its perpetuation. Stringent enforcement of the policy and purpose of the Act may serve to educate public opinion better.

(a) A very small but significant step could be taken by the Government by declaring the taking and giving of dowry to be against the Government Servants' Conduct Rules. Such a lead was given earlier to prevent bigamous marriages and giving or taking of dowry should be similarly dealt with (4.78).

(b) The policy of making the offence non-cognisable nullifies the purpose of the Act. We recommended that the offences under the Dowry Act should be made cognisable (4.80).

(c) One of the major loop-holes in the existing legislation is that anything is allowed in the name of gifts and presents. Therefore, any gifts made to the bridegroom or his parents in excess of Rs. 500 or which can be so used as to reduce his own financial liability should be made punishable (4.81).

(d) The practice of displaying the Dowry tends to perpetuate the practice as others follow suit. To curb the evil of dowry we recommend legislation on the lines of the West Pakistan Dowry (Prohibition of Display) Act, 1967 which penalised display of gifts made at the time or immediately before or after marriage (4.82).

(e) An evaluation of the impact of the amended Dowry Prohibition Act should be made after 5 years. The next step should be to set a ceiling even on the gifts that may be made to the bride (4.83).

8. Improvement of Laws of Divorce

The concept of 'union for life' or the sacramental nature of marriage which renders the marriage indissoluble has gradually been eroded and through legislation the right on divorce has been introduced in all legal systems in India, but the same variations and unequal treatment of sexes characterises this branch of law also (4.84).

We Recommended the Following Changes

Hindu Law:

(a) difference in the place of work should not be regarded as a ground for a case of desertion or restitution of conjugal rights (4.94).

(b) cruelty and desertion should be added as grounds for divorce in the Hindu Marriage Act so that persons are not compelled to follow the present circuitous route and undergo the expense of going to court twice (4.95).

Muslim Law:

(c) We recommend that the right of the wife to divorce on the failure of the husband to maintain her, irrespective of her conduct which may be the main or contributory cause, should be clearly spelt out (4.100).

(d) We recommend immediate legislation to eliminate the unilateral right of divorce, and to introduce parity of rights for both partners regarding grounds for seeking dissolution of a marriage (4.103).

Christian Law: (e) We regret that the reforms in Christian Marriage laws as recommended by the Law Commission and incorporated in the Christian Marriage Matrimonial Causes Bill 1960 have not yet been enacted and recommend that no further time be lost to reform and amend this law (4.104-4.106).

Jewish Law: (f) We recommend that reform and codification on the Jewish law be undertaken and the principle of monogamy as well as the normal grounds for divorce as provided in the Special Marriage Act be adopted for this community also (4.108).

General

(g) In our opinion conversion should not be a ground for divorce as it offers an easy way of avoiding matrimonial obligations (4.111).

(h) We recommend that mutual consent as a ground for divorce should be recognised in all the personal laws so that two adults whose marriage has, in fact, broken down can get it dissolved honourably (4.112).

(i) The provision in the Parsee Marriage and Divorce Act which enables the wife to obtain a divorce if her husband has compelled her to prostitution should be included in all other personal laws (4.113).

(j) As a general principle, we recommend parity of rights regarding grounds for divorce for both husband and wife (4.114).

9. Adoption

(a) We recommend that the right of adoption should be equal for husband and wife, with the consent of the other spouse (4.125).

(b) We welcome the step taken by the Government in introducing a uniform and secular law of adoption, the adoption of Children Bill, 1972, and recommend and early enactment of the Bill as it will extend the right of adoption, equally to men and women of all communities, and will be a step towards a uniform secular law (4.129).

10. Guardianship

We recommend:

(a) that the control over the person and property of minor cannot be separated and should vest in the same person;

(b) that the question of guardianship should be determined entirely from the point of view of the child's interest and not the prior right of either parent;

(c) that the parent who does not have guardianship should have access to the child.

(d) that whatever the decision taken earlier, the child's choice of guardian should be obtained when the child reaches the age of 12 (4.143).

(e) We support the recommendations of the U.N. Commission on the Status of Women as follows:

(i) Women shall have equal right and duties with men in respect to guardianship of their minor children and the exercise of parental authority over them, including care, custody, education and maintenance;

(ii) Both spouses shall have equal rights and duties with regard to the administration of the property of their minor children, with the legal limitations necessary to ensure as far as possible that it is administered in the interest of the children;

(iii) The interest of the children shall be the paramount consideration in proceedings custody of children in the event of divorce, annulment of marriages or judicial separation;

(iv) No discrimination shall be made between men and women with regard to decisions regarding custody of children and guardianship or other parental rights in the event of divorce, annulment of marriage or judicial separation (4.144).

11. Maintenance

The provision for maintenance in the Criminal Procedure Code continues to reflect the old attitude to women. With some modifications like extending the rights to demand maintenance to indigent parents and to divorced wives, the obligation to maintain continues to be that of the man. There are today women economically independent who cannot only look after themselves but also their husband and children (4.147).

(a) As we believe in the equal status of husband and wife, and of son and daughter, we recommend amendment of the law of maintenance to provide for the obligation of the economically independent women:

  (i) to maintain her dependent husband;

  (ii) to share with him the duty to maintain their children;

  (iii) to share with her brothers the duty to maintain their indigent parents (4.148).

(b) The underlying principle for the inclusion of the right of maintenance in the Criminal Procedure Code is to prevent starvation and vagarancy. The ceiling of Rs. 500 on the total amount of maintenance for all dependent persons seems unjustified (4.148).

In extending the right of maintenance to divorced wives, an exception has been introduced to deny maintenance to those divorced wives who have received a sum of money payable under customary or personal law. This exclusion of all divorced Muslim women defeats the purpose of the section to provide a speedy remedy to indigent women (4.149).

We therefore recommend that the ceiling placed on the maximum amount payable as maintenance should be removed and the term 'wife to include divorced wife be made applicable to all women without any exception (4.150).

(c) Under Muslim law the wife's right to maintenance lasts only as long as she remains a wife. If she is divorced, she loses her right and is only entitled to maintenance for 3 months. This has created a discrimination between the Muslim and other Indian women. We recommend the removal of this discrimination and extension of right of maintenance to divorced wives (4.155).

(d) In order to minimise the hardship caused by non-payment of maintenance, and to ensure certainly of payment, we recommend that all maintenance orders should be deducted at the source by the employer as done in the case of income-tax. Where it is not possible to deduct at the source, as in the case of a business man or a self-employed person, the arrears of maintenance should be recovered as 'arrears of land revenue or by distress' (4.159).

(e) An additional mode of execution of the maintenance degree may be to adopt the same procedure as is done in the case of fines under the Criminal Procedure Code (4.160).

12. Inheritance

(a) The Indian Succession Act confers no restrictions on the power of a person to will away his property. Therefore, the protection enjoyed by a Muslim widow to a share of the estate and by a Hindu widow to be maintained is denied to other widows under this law. There is a need to incorporate some restruction on the right of testation, similar to that prevailing under Muslim law to prevent a widow from being left completely destitute (4.165).

(b) A characteristic feature of the Travancore and Cochin Christian Succession Laws is the discrimination against women (4.167). We recommend that immediate legislative measures be taken to bring Christian women of Kerala under the Indian Succession Act as a first step to unify the law (4.173).

(c) According to the law prevailing in Goa, the widow' is relegated to the fourth position and is entitled to only the fruits and agricultural commodities. This needs to be remedied immediately (4.177). Similar anomalies prevail in the succession laws governing Christians of Pondicherry which relegate a woman to an inferior position and do not regard her as full owner even in the few cases where she can inherit property (4.178). We recommend the extension of the Indian Succession Act to Goa and Pondicherry (4.178).

(d) The one major factor which helps to continue the inequality between sons and daughters under Hindu law is the retention of the Mitakshara co-parcenary, the membership of which is confined only to male members. A number of decisions and legislation in the 20th century have made inroads in the concept of the co-parcenary, but the suggestion regarding its abolition received opposition at the time of Hindu Law reform. The compromise arrived at provides limited inheritance rights to the nearest class I female heirs of a co-parcenary but perpetuate unequal treatment between brother and sister. The right of a co-parcenar to renounce his share in the co-parcenary deprives the female heirs of any share. Secondly, the right to transform self-acquired into joint family property is frequently used to reduce the share of a female heir (4.189-4.193).

We recommend the abolition of the right by birth and the conversion of the Mitakshara co-parcenary into Dayabhaga (4.194).

(e) Section 4 (2) of the Hindu Succession Act, excludes the devolution of tenancy rights under State laws from the scope of the Act. This had led to the elimination of the beneficial effects of the Hindu Succession Act under the land legislation in many States (4.195-200). In order to achieve the social equality of women as also in the interests of uniformity, we recommend the abolition of the exception provided in section 4 (2) of the Hindu Succession Act, relating to devolution of tenancies (4.201).

(f) Section 23 of the Hindu Succession Act relating to the right of inheritance to a dwelling house has also resulted in some discrimination between unmarried, widowed and married daughters. The main object of the section is unexceptionalble as it asserts the primacy of the rights of the family as against the right of an individual and therefore the restriction against partition which is against the family interest should be retained. But nothing justifies the indivious distinction between married and other daughters (4.204 and 4.205). We recommend the removal of the discrimination between married and unmarried daughters regarding the right over a dwelling house (Sec. 23 Hindu Succession Act).

(g) The unrestricted right of testation often results in depriving female heirs of their rights of inheritance (4.206). We recommend that the right of testation should be limited under the Hindu Succession Act, so as not to deprive legal heirs completely (4.207).

(h) We recommend legislation in Muslim Law to give an equal share to the widow and the daughter along with sons as has been done in Turkey (4.218).

(i) The medley of laws which govern the right of inheritance, not only of female heirs of different communities; but even of female heirs of the same community require immediate measures. Broad principles like equal rights of sons, daughters and widows, a restriction on the right of testation, so that dependent members are not left completely destitute are needed immediately (4.219).

GENERAL RECOMMENDATIONS

13. Matrimonial Property

In the socio-economic situation prevailing in our country the contribution of the wife to the family's economy is not recognised. A large number of them participate in the family's effort to earn a livelihood as unpaid family workers. Even when they do not do so the economic value of their effort in running the house, assuming all domestic responsibilities, thus freeing the husband for his avocation is not accepted in law either directly or indirectly. Married women who do not have independent source of income or give up employment after marriage to devote their full time in family obligations are economically dependent on their husbands. In majority of cases, movable and immovable property acquired during marriage are legally owned by the husband, since they are paid for out of his earnings. The principle of determining ownership on the basis of financial contribution works inequitably against women. In case of divorce or separation, women without any earnings or savings of their own are deprived of all property which they acquire jointly. Even property received by them at the time of marriage from the husband or his family is denied to the women in some communities. The fear of financial and social insecurity prevents them from restoring to separation or divorce even when the marriages are unhappy. It is necessary to give legal recognition to the economic value of the contribution made by the wife through house work for purposes of determining ownership of matrimonial property, instead of continuing the archaic test of actual financial contribution (4.222-4.225).

We, therefore recommend that on divorce or separation the wife should be entitled to at least 1/3 of the assets acquired at the time of and during the marriage (4.226).

14. Family Courts

The statutory law in all matrimonial matters follows the adversary principle for giving relief i.e. the petitioner seeking relief alleges certain facts and the respondent refutes them. In addition, most of the grounds in these statutes are based on the 'fault principle' instead of the breakdown theory. As a result, strong advocacy rather than family welfare is often the determining factor in these cases. The absence of distinction between matrimonial causes and other civil suits leads to unusual delay which stands in the ways of conciliation and further embitters the relationship of the parties. Conciliation, which needs to be the main consideration in all family matters is not the guiding principle in the statutes dealing with them (4.227-4.228).

We strongly recommend the abandonment of the established adversary system for settlement of family problems, and establishment of Family Courts which will adopt conciliatory methods and informal procedure, aiming to achieve socially desirable results (4.233).

15. Uniform Civil Code

The absence of an uniform civil code 27 years after independence is an incongruity which cannot be justified with all the emphasis that is placed on secularism, science and modernisation. The continuance of various personal laws which discriminate between men and women violates the Fundamental Rights and the Preamble to the Constitution which promises equality of status to all citizens. It is also against the spirit of national integration and secularism (4.236).

Our recommendations regarding amendments of existing laws are only indicators of the direction in which uniformity has to be achieved. We recommend expeditious implementation of the constitutional directive of Article 44 by the adoption of a uniform Civil Code (4.237).

16. Needed Reforms in Criminal Law

(a) *Consent to sexual intercourse:* While consent to sexual intercourse is strictly interpreted and excludes consent given by the woman under duress or fraud, no provision is made for consent obtained by putting someone else in fear in the presence of the woman. We welcome the recommendation of the Law Commission in this regard (4.242).

In our view consent to have sexual intercourse requires more maturity than to have an abortion. The same age-limit should be applied in both cases. We recommended that the age of consent below which a girl's consent to sexual intercourse is not legal should be 18, permitting some degree of flexibility to the court in border-line cases to decide whether the girl is mature enough (4.243).

(b) *Bigamy:* The present law restricts jurisdiction of the court to the place where the bigamous marriage was performed or where the husband and wife last resided. This causes difficulties to the wife who may have to move on after being abandoned by her husband. We recommend that in addition to the two jurisdictions under the Criminal Procedure Code, provision be made for inquiry and trial for bigamy in a court within whose jurisdiction the wife is residing (4.246).

(c) *Adultery:* Adultery in our opinion should be regarded only as a matrimonial offence, the remedy for which may be sought in divorce or separation. Retention of this as a criminal offence brings out clearly the values of the last century which regarded the wife as the husband's property. It also prevents lawyers and others from giving necessary help to an oppressed wife. We recommend that continuing to regard adultery as a criminal offence is against the dignity of an individual and should be removed from the Penal Code (4.248).

17. Nationality

(a) In the absence of any provision dealing with the case of Indian women marrying foreigners in the Citizenship Act many of them have become stateless. We recommend that the Citizenship Act be amended to provide a special rule for Indian women marrying aliens, stating that she will in no case lose her Indian nationality as a result of her marriage to a foreigner (4.256).

(b) The present rule prevents the children of such Indian women from being considered as Indian citizens. Where the father and mother are separated and the mother is the guardian, there is no justification for the rule that the child's' nationality will be transmitted through the father. We, therefore, recommend the amendment of section 4 (1) of the Citizenship Act to read as follows:

> "A person born outside India on or after the 26th January, 1950, shall be a citizen of India by descent if his father or mother is a citizen of India at the time of his birth" (4.257).

CHAPTER V—ROLES, RIGHTS AND OPPORTUNITIES FOR ECONOMIC PARTICIPATION

The Indian Constitution guarantees equality of opportunity in matters relating to employment and directs the State to secure equal rights to an adequate means of livelihood, equal pay for equal work and just and humane conditions of work. The impact of transition to a modern economy has meant the exclusion of a increasing number and proportion of women from active participation in the productive process. A considerable number continue to participate for no return and no recognition. The majority of those who do participate fully or on sufferance, without equal treatment, security of employment or humane conditions of work, a very large number of them are subject to exploitation of various kinds with no protection from society or the State. Legislative and executive actions initiated in this direction have made some impact in the organised sector, where only 6% of working women are employed, but in the vast unorganised sector, which engages 94% of working women in this country, no impact of these measures have been felt on conditions of work, wages or opportunities.

Estimates of employment and under-employment clearly indicate that the position is worse for women. Measures to remove women's disability and handicaps in the field of economic participation have proved extremely inadequate. While several factors have handicapped and prevented women's integration into the process of development, the lack of a well defined policy, indicating areas where they require special assistance and protection, leaves them without access to knowledge, skills and employment.

Prejudices regarding women's' efficiency, productivity, capacity for skills and suitability debar them from employment in many areas, and result in wage discrimination. The criteria for determining their unsuitability for particular types of jobs are not clear or uniform. Recasting the employment policy for women requires re-examination of existing theories regarding their suitability for different types of work on scientific lines, and deliberate efforts to promote equality of opportunity by special attention to women's disability and handicaps. Our recommendations aim to make the Constitutional guarantees meaningful and arrest the trend toward gradual exclusion of women from their rights to a fuller participation in the economic process.

18. We therefore recommend the adoption of a well defined policy to fulfil the Constitutional directives and Government's long-term objective of total involvement of women in national development. Such a policy should be framed by a Government Resolution. This policy will need to be implemented carefully to avoid evasion by direction or indirect methods. Apart from specific occupations from which women are debarred by laws, employers should not be permitted to exclude them from any occupation unless the basis for unsuitability is clearly specified.

19. The creation of a cell within the Ministry of Labour and Employment at both Central and State levels under the direction of a Senior Officer to deal with problems of women (5.323).

We further recommend the following changes in the existing laws:

20A. Maternity Benefits Act 1961

(i) This Act should be extended to all industries not covered by the Act at present and the provision of maternity relief ensured by the creation of a Central Fund levying contributions from employers. The administration of the Fund should follow the pattern already established by the Employees State Insurance Corporation.

(ii) The Act should also cover agricultural labourers in the same manner as suggested for other industries. To facilitate its implementation, the Central Fund should also include a levy on Agricultural Holdings Tax by the Committee on Taxation of Agricultural Wealth and Income.

(iii) The anti-reterchment clause already included in the Employees State Insurance Act 1948 should be incorporated in the Maternity Benefits Act.

(iv) For women retrenched for short periods and reemployed on the same jobs, the period of unemployment should not be treated as discontinuation of service for their eligibility for this benefit. For casual labour, a minimum of 3 months of service should be considered as qualifying them for this benefit.

(v) As decided by the Supreme Court in the case of bidi workers, the provision of maternity benefits should be extended to home workers in all other industries.

(vi) In order to eliminate unjust denial of maternity benefits, scrutiny of applications should be done by a Committee of the management and trade union representatives. The latter should preferably include a women. This will provide greater incentive to women workers to participate in trade union activities.

(vii) The penalties for evasion of this law should be made more stringent.

(viii) The system of paying cash benefits in a lumpsum sometimes gives rise to inadequate attention to the nutritional needs of the mother and the child. Payment of maternity benefits should be made periodically (5.324).

21B. Provision of Creches

(i) The present limit of 50 women workers for the application of this provision under the Factories Act should be reduced to 20.

(ii) Women employed as casual labour or as contract labour should be entitled to share this benefit.

(iii) Wherever there is a demand, a room should be provided for keeping small children for other group of women workers e.g. workers in offices, hospitals, shops and commercial establishments.

(iv) As far as possible, creches should be established near the residence of women workers rather than the place of work. The ideal arrangements, in our view, would be nieighbourhood creches (5.325).

22C. Working Time

Permission to work upto 10.00 P.M. should be granted, provided arrangements for transport and security are made.

23. We further recommend effective implementation of the Maternity Benefits Act in all States, and the extension of the Employees State Insurance Scheme to those areas which are not covered by it at present (5.326).

24. Equalisation of Wages

We recommend legislative enactment of Article 39 (d) of the Constitution—equal pay for equal work—to add the weight of legal sanction to what is only a policy at present.

We further recommend incorporation of this principle in the Minimum Wages Act (5.327).

25. Integrated Development of Training and Employment

(i) We recommend reservation of a definite quota for women for training within the industry in order to arrest their retrenchment as a consequence of modernisation.

(ii) A similar quota should be reserved for women for training of apprentices under the National Apprentices Act.

(iii) We further recommend development programme of vocational training in close relationship with industries and resources located in the area. Links with possible employing agencies have to be develop from the beginning so that the training does not end in futility.

(iv) As recommended by the Committee of the All India Council for Technical Education, Polytechnics for Women should include a production centre with assistance from the Small Scale Industries Departments of the State concerned.

(v) Training programmes in production and market organisation to develop self employment should be developed.

(vi) Special efforts have to be made to develop vocational training for both illiterate and semi-literate women workers.

(vii) We further recommend development of training-cum-production centres in small-scale or cottage industries in both rural and urban areas to provide employment to women near their homes (5.328).

26. Part-time Employment

We recommend specific provision for part-time employment of women by suitable revisions in recruitment rules and service conditions. We also recommend detailed investigation of areas where part-time employment could be generated by agencies like the Directorate General of Employment and Training, the Institute of Applied Manpower Research, the National Council of Applied Economic Research, etc. Such studies should include examination of existing avenues for part-time employment viz. in the unorganised industries and occupations (5.329).

27. *Employment Information*

We recommend expansion of the national employment service, particularly in rural areas, and the development of a women's cadre in the service to provide employment information and assistance to women (5.330).

28. *Provision for Re-entry*

We recommend that provision for special leave without pay, subject to a maximum of 5 years during service, should be made in all occupations, in order to enable women to devote full-time for the care of their family. Their lien should be protected (5.331).

29. *Enforcement of Laws Protection Women Workers*

We recommend increase in the number of women on the inspectorate different labour departments as well as provision for women welfare officers wherever women are employed (5.332).

30. *We Further Recommend*

(i) Steps to organise labour unions in the field of agriculture, and other industries where such organisations do not exist at present.

(ii) Formation of Women's Wings in all trade unions, to look after the problems of women workers and to improve women's participation in trade union activities (5.333).

CHAPTER VI—EDUCATIONAL DEVELOPMENT

Our investigation of the progress of women's education in India reveals that while there has been a tremendous increase in the number of girls receiving formal education in the period after Independence the gap between the enrolment of boys and girls has continued to increase at all levels and the proportion of girls in the relevant age-groups covered by the school system still remains far below the constitutional target of universal education upto the age at 14. Social attitude to the education of girls range from acceptance of the need to one of the absolute in difference. The reasons for the variation in social attitude and the consequent slow progress of women's education are both social and economic, which are intensified by inadequate facilities and the ambivalent attitude regarding the purpose of educating girls.

In spite of the expansion, the formal system of education now covers only 10% of the total female population. Less than 7% of the 15 to 25 age-group and less than 2% of the 25 and above age-group have received any formal education. The number of illiterate women has increased from 61 million in 1950-51 to 215 million in 1970-71.

31. The challenge of the widening illiteracy gap will have to be borne in mind in determining priorities in educational development in the years to come. The claims of the formal educational system which can cater to the need of only a minority for a long time will have to be balanced against the claims of eradication of illiteracy. This stand out as the most important and imperative need to raise the status of women who are already adults and constitute the largest group (6.53). While the constitutional directive of universal education upto the age of 14 must receive the highest priority in the formal system.....an alternative system has to be designed to provide basic education to adult women, particularly in the 15-25 age-group (6.55).

Imbalances in women's education and literacy are the consequences of great disparity of educational progress between rural and urban areas, between different sections of the population and between regions, which reflect, to a great extent, variations in regional attitudes to women (6.57). The influences of these and other sociological factors, which, for instance, influence the low educational development among Muslim women or women of Scheduled Castes and Tribes.....make the use of national or state averages in assessing progress of education or literacy rather meaningless (6.61-63).

32. In our opinion, any plan for educational development of women which does not take these imbalances into account will contribute to the increase of inequalities between different sections of the population. Removal of these imbalances will require special attention from public authorities based on careful identification of factors responsible for them. Special programmes will need to be designed for their removal if equality of educational opportunities is to be brought within the access of the majority of women in this country (6.64).

Recommendations Regarding the Formal System

33. Co-education

In our opinion, the considerations of efficiency, economy as well as equal opportunity require the acceptance of co-education as a long term policy. In view of the divergent social attitudes, however, we recommend:

(i) Co-education should be adopted as the general policy at the primary level;

(ii) At the middle and secondary stages separate schools may be provided in areas where there is a great demand for them. But the effort to pursue co-education as a general policy at these stages should continue side-by-side;

(iii) At the university level-co-education should be the general policy and opening of new colleges exclusively for girls should be discouraged;

(iv) There should be no ban on admission of girls to boys' institutions;

(v) Wherever separate schools/colleges for girls are provided, it has to be ensured that they maintain required standards in regard to the quality of staff, provision of facilities, relevant courses and co-curricular activities;

(vi) Acceptance of the principle of mixed staff should be made a condition of recognition for mixed schools. There is a misgiving, however, that this provision may lead to exclusion of girls from some schools. Therefore, it is suggested that this measures may be reviewed a few years after it is implemented;

(vii) Wherever there are mixed schools, separate toilet facilities and retiring rooms for girls should be provided (6.72).

34. Curricula

We recommend:

(i) There should be a common course of general education for both sexes till the end of class X, all courses being open to boys and girls.

(ii) At the primary stage, simple needle craft, music and dancing should be taught to both sexes.

(iii) From the middle stage, differences may be permitted under work experience.

(iv) In class XI-XII girls should have full opportunity to choose vocational and technical courses according to local conditions, needs and aptitudes.

(v) At the university stage there is a need to introduce more relevant and useful courses for all students (6.81).

35. Pre-School Education

We recommend:

(i) The provision of three years pre-school education for all children by making a special effort to increase the number of 'balwadis' in the rural areas and in urban slums.

(ii) In order to enable them to fulfil the social functions discussed above, an effort should be made to locate them as near as possible to the primary and middle schools of the locality (6.85).

36. Universalisation of Education for the Age-Group 6.14

We recommend:

(i) Provision of primary schools within walking distance from the home of every child within the next 5 years.

(ii) Establishment of ashram or residential schools to serve clusters of villages scattered in difficult terrains. Where this is not immediately possible, preparatory schools may be provided for the time being.

(iii) Provision of mobile schools for children of nomadic tribes, migrant labour and construction workers.

(iv) Sustained propaganda by all types of persons, preferably women-officials, and non-officials, social and political workers, to bring every girl into school in Class I preferably at the age of 6. They should visit local schools and involve parents and community leaders in order to promote the schooling of girls, particularly in backward areas.

(v) Provision of incentives to drop-outs. Since poverty is the major cause of drop-outs the most effective incentive, in our opinion is the provision of mid-day meals. The rate of children passing the primary level has definitely gone up in States which have introduced mid-day meals. In Kerala, which has the highest literacy rate among women, this provision is one of the major factors for the enrolment and retention of children in schools to-day. In reply to our questionnaire, the majority has given highest priority to this incentive. The other important incentives which require to the provided to needy children are free school uniforms, scholarships or stipends and free supply of books and other study material. For girls particularly, the lack of adequate clothing is a great deterrent to attending schools. For schools which do not prescribe any uniform, some provision of clothing is necessary.

(vi) Special incentives for areas where enrolment of girls is low. This will need to be worked out according to local conditions. We suggest special awards or recognition to the community, teachers, students etc.

(vii) At least 50% of teachers at this stage should be women.

(viii) Provision of at least two teachers in all schools, and conversion of the existing single teacher ones as early as possible.

(ix) Developing a system of part-time education for girls who cannot attend school on a full-time basis. This system should provide education to girls at a time convenient to them.

(x) Adoption of the multiple entry system for girls who could not attend school earlier or had to leave before becoming functionally literate.

(xi) Provision of additional space in schools so that girls

can bring their younger brothers and sisters to be looked after, either by the girls themselves in turn, or by some local women (6.87).

(xii) Opening of schools and greater flexibility in admission procedure in middle schools (multiple only), to help girls to complete their schooling (6.88).

37. Sex Education

We recommend:

(i) Introduction of sex education from middle school.

(ii) Appointment of an expert group by the Ministry of Education to prepare graded teaching material on the subject. The group should include some experts on mass media, to advise on the use of films and other mass media for this purpose.

(iii) This material may be used for both formal and non-formal education (6.89).

38. Secondary Education

We recommend:

(i) Free education for all girls up to the end of the secondary stage.

(ii) Improving the quality of teaching and provision of facilities for important subject like science, mathematics and commerce.

(iii) Introduction of job-oriented work experience, keeping in view the needs, the resources and the employment potential of the region e.g. courses leading to training as ANM, typing and commercial practice, programmes oriented to industry and simple technology, agriculture and animal husbandry (6.92).

39. General Recommendations

(i) Provision of mixed staff in all mixed schools. This should be made a condition of recognition.

(ii) Adequate provision of common-rooms and separate toilet facilities for girls in all schools.

(iii) Adequate arrangements for co-curricular activities for girls in all schools.

(iv) Provision of more need-cum-merit scholarships and hostel facilities for girls (6.93).

40. Higher Education

We recommend:

(i) Development of more employment opportunities, particularly of a part-time nature, to enable women to participate more in productive activities.

(ii) Development of employment information and guidance services for women entering higher education. Many of them suffer from lack of information regarding job opportunities and regret their choice of subjects when faced by difficulties in obtaining employment (6.96).

41. Non-Formal Education

As stated earlier, the greatest problem in women's education today is to provide some basic education to the overwhelming majority who have remained outside the reach of the formal system because of their age and social responsibilities as well as the literacy gap. For the sake of national plans for development, it is imperative to increase the social effectiveness of women in the 15-25 age-group even if we cannot do so for the still older groups. Ad hoc approaches through the adult literacy, functional literacy and other programmes of the Government have provide inadequate. They also draw a sharp distinction between men and women in the content of the training. These distinctions, in our view, are out of date. Changes in family life, food habits, family planning all require joint efforts of men and women and continuing this kind of artificial division between the sexes may defeat the purpose of these programmes. As for vocational and occupational skills, the needs of women are greater than those of men. While we do not deny the value of crafts, women's need for vocational training cannot be limited to them. The skills differ according to the industrial and market potentials of regions and it is imperative to relate the training to local needs, resources and employment possibilities instead of adopting an artificial sex-selective approach. Ad hoc approaches through a multiplicity of programmes by various governmental agencies will lead to overlapping, lack of coordination and wastage of resources. The problem is an integrated one and cannot be solved by short-term programmes. What is needed is a continuous process (6.97-6.101).

No attempt to professionalise this system will lead to development of the limiting, selective and a rigid approach with fixed curricula and classroom procedures. The prohibitive cost of such professionalisation would inevitably limit its operation to a few selected centres. The teachers in a non-formal system must have other skills of direct relevance to the problems of the community. Without this kind of community involvement, such programmes will lack stability and continuity (6.104).

The object of the system should be to provide access to information and use of information for better participation in social life with literacy as the ore of the package. Though primarily meant for adolescents, the system should not exclude the young, particularly those who have been a denied any formal education. Some of the latter may use it as a stepping stone to enter the formal system if our recommendation regarding multiple entry is accepted (6.105-6.106).

The system will have to be organised through community groups. The Panchayats and the Women's Panchayats recommended in Chapter VII would appear to be the ideal bodies for this purpose. Government's role should be limited to providing technical guidance and advice and enabling Government functionaries at the local level to participate in the programme apart from supporting assistance in the form of literature and reading material. Development of basic libraries in villages and the slum areas of towns is an imperative necessity for this purpose. We therefore recommend concentration of governmental effort on providing this infrastructure (6.107).

42. *Equality of Sexes as a Major Value to be Inculcated Through the Educational Process*

The educational system is the only institution which can counteract traditional belief in inequality of sexes. The educational system today has not even attempted to undertake this responsibility. The schools reflect and strengthen the traditional prejudices through their curricula, classification of subjects on the basis of sex and the unwritten code of conduct enforced on their pupils. This is one area where a major change is needed in the content and organisation of education. Educators must admit their responsibility and bring about this much needed change in the values of the younger generation (6.108-111).

CHAPTER VII—POLITICAL STATUS

Though women's participation in the political process has increased, both in election and in their readiness to express their views on issues directly concerning their day-to-day life, their ability to produce an impact on the political process has been negligible because of the inadequate attention paid to their political education and mobilisation by both political parties and women's organisations. Parties have tended to see women voters as appendages of the males. Among women, the leadership has become diffused and diverse-with sharp contradictions in their regard and concern for the inequalities that affect the status of women in every sphere-social, economic and political. The revolution in status of women for which constitutional equality was to be only the instrument, still remains a very distant objective. While the position of some groups have changed for the better, the large masses of women continue to lack spokesmen in the representative bodies of the State. Though women do not constitute a minority numerically, they are acquiring the features of one by the inequality of class, status and political power. In this sense the new rights have proved to be only concessional. Our recommendations aim to make women's political rights more functional as required by the needs of a democratic system (7.95-101).

In order to provide greater opportunities to women to actively participate in the decision-making process, it is imperative to recognise the true nature of the social inequalities and disabilities that hamper them. This can best be achieved by providing them with special opportunities for participation in the representative structure of local government*. The present form of associating women in these bodies, through cooption or nomination has become a kind of tokenism. The time has come to move out of this token provision to a more meaningful association of women in local administration, and to counteract the general apathy and indifference of the local bodies to women's development and change of status (7.115-6).

43. Women's Panchayats

We therefore recommend the establishment of Statutory Women's Panchayats at the village level with autonomy and resources of their own for the management and administration of welfare and development programmes for women and children, as a transitional measure, to break through the traditional attitudes that inhibit most women from articulating their problems are participating actively in the existing local bodies. They should be directly elected by the women of the village and have the right to send representatives to the Panchayat Samities and/or Zilla Parishads. A viable relationship with the Gram Panchayats should be maintained by making the Chairman and Secretary of both bodies ex-officio members of the other.

*44. Reservation of Municipalities***

At the level of municipalities, the principle of reservation of seats for women is already prevalent in certain States. We, therefore, recommend that this should be adopted by all States as a transitional measure. We also recommend the constitution of permanent committees in municipalities, to initiate and supervise programmes for women's welfare and development.

45. Policy for Political Parties

We recommend that political parties should adopt as definite policy regarding the percentage of women candidates to be sponsored by them for elections to Parliament and State Assemblies. While they may initially start with 15 per cent. This should be gradually increased so that in time to come the representation of women in the legislative bodies has some relationship to their position in the total population of the country or the State.

46. Association in Important Bodies

We further recommend the inclusion of women in all important committees, commission or delegations that are appointed to examine socio-economic problems.

CHAPTER VIII—POLICIES AND PROGRAMMES FOR WOMEN'S WELFARE AND DEVELOPMENT

47. Health and Family Planning

Demographic indicators. viz, female, maternal and infant mortality rates, and indicators of access to medical care, both reveal an increase in the neglect of female lives as an expendable asset. This is the only reasonable explanation for the declining sex ratio observed to persist over several decades. In our opinion, the neglect of maternity and child health serves and general public health services through over-concentration on efforts for family planning have contributed to this trend as well as defeated the ultimate objective of the family planning programme. We are entirely in agreement with the draft Fifth Five-Year Plan that integration of family planning with more positive health services like maternal and child health, and nutrition and improvement in the life expectancy of children and mothers will provide a far greater incentive to the adoption of family planning measures than the hitherto adopted negative approach. While welcoming this proposed integration, we with to offer certain suggestions wish regard to its organisation at different levels so that the objective of integration is not defeated by organisational separatism (8.117).

We recommend that:

(a) The rank of the Chief Executive for the integrated maternity and child health services, including family planning, should be upgraded to at least Additional Commissioner, so that this service does not again become subordinate to family planning. This procedure should be adopted at all levels of the administration at the Centre and the States.

(b) A separate budget head for maternity and child health services should be created, drawing on the provision now made for family planning and the general health services. It is important to increase the provision for these services to avoid their being neglected as has been the trend so far. Since programmes for immunisation and nutrition of infants yield better results when they form a part of general maternity and child health services, we see no difficulty in increasing the allocation for these services.

(c) At the level of the primary health centres, the maternity and child health service should be separated for purposes of administrative provision, medical personnel and budget. While they may share the same buildings and equipment, a separation of the administrative structure required for maternity and child health services will ensure greater priority of treatment. Facilities in the way of maternity beds, equipment for immunisation of children and family planning for women could be allocated to the MCH Unit. The P.H.C. could be made responsible for sterilisation operations for men along with other general health services.

The MCH Unit could coordinate the nutrition and immunisation measures which form a basis component of the integrated child development programme. It could also collect and maintain fertility and morbidity statistics for women and children for better research and evaluation in these fields.

We recommend that each M.C.H. centre should collect this data which should be studied and evaluated at the district level by persons of required competence. This will call for a health statistics Section at the district level.

(d) We recommend the abolition of the present practice of providing financial incentives to promoters of family planning. Incentives to women who accept family planning should be in the shape of a token or certificate to ensure them greater priority in health care facilities for both the mothers and their children. Such a step will promote greater acceptance of family planning and correct social attitudes towards these practices. Compensation for loss of wages during sterilisation operations should however be paid to daily wage labourers. Others should be given paid leave for this purpose.

(e) The qualifications prescribed for recruitment of personnel for these services in rural areas need to be gradually raised. Unit women of requisite higher qualifications are available, the present requirements may continue, but they should be reviewed and progressively increased after every 3 years. Attempts should also be made to obtain the services of older and mature women for these services in the rural areas.

(f) We further recommend the promotion of research in the field of female disorders e.g. puerperal psychosis and effects of family planning methods.

(g) We disapprove the denial of maternity benefits to women in Government service after three children as adopted by some State Government and recommend rescinding of such orders.

(h) We also recommend that mass campaigns for family planning should also aim to correct prevailing social attitudes regarding fertility and metabolic hereditary disorders and the sex of the child for which the women is generally blamed. Correct information in these matters would go a long way to improve the status of women (8.177).

48. Changes Needed in the Medical Termination of Pregnancy Act

(a) According to Section 4 (a) of the Act, consent of a minor girl is not required for this operation while in other surgical operations of children above 12 such consent is necessary. In our view this distinction is uncalled for and may lead to guardians compelling young girls to undergo this operation even when they do not want it. The consent of the patient should be essential. In the case of a minor girl nearing majority, if the doctor and the patient are in agreement, the consent of the guardian may be dispensed with. In all such cases, greater discretion should be permitted to the doctor (8.85).

(b) Sections 8 of the Act provides an overriding precaution to the doctor for any damage caused by the operation. Since no such protection is given for other operations, this seems an unnecessary clause and may lead to negligence. It may, therefore, be dropped (8.85).

(c) While we appreciate the ethical considerations which make many doctors reluctant to perform this operation, we feel that it is a woman's right to have control over the size of her family. At the same time it is important that doctors should have the authority to discourage such operations when they pose definite risk to the health of a patient. The condition being imposed in many hospitals that abortion will only be performed if the patient agrees to sterilisation, should not be compulsive. it would be far better to adopt methods of persuasion through expert counselling (8.80-81).

(d) The procedure and paper work involved in these operations need to be simplified. It is also necessary to extend facilities for authorised termination of pregnancies, particularly in the rural areas (8.83).

(e) Many hospitals continue to insist on the husband's consent before performing these operations though this is not required by the law. A special effort needs to be made to convince the medical profession of the social value of this law from the point of view both individuals and society (8.83).

(f) Most doctors are reluctant to perform these operations in the case of unmarried girls. It is necessary to clarify the point that rape is not the only ground to justify termination in cases of unmarried girls, nor is there any legal obligation on the doctor to inform the Policy of an operation done in a rape case (8.84).

B. Welfare and Development

49. In order to prevent any ambiguity in the understanding of what constitutes women's welfare and to prevent the development of policies that sometimes go against the basic objectives, we recommend that the Government of India should evolve a national policy on women's development in the light of the constitutional directives and pledges made to the women of this country and to the international community from time to time (89.178).

50. In view of the need to maintain links between

governmental, voluntary and community effort for promotion of women's welfare and to assist the process of Government planning with actual knowledge and experiences of the problems and needs of women at different levels.

We recommend:

(a) Reorganisation of the Central Social Welfare Board as a statutory and autonomous specialised agency for planning, coordination and management of welfare and development programmes for women and children.

(b) Reorganisation of the State Welfare Advisory Boards as statutory autonomous agencies at the State level with similar functions. In addition, the State Boards may also serve as links between the Central agency, the State Government and the local bodies.

51. Need for Agencies for Coordination, Communication and Implementation of Measures to Improve the Status of Women (Note After Chapter IX)

The U.N. Commission on the Status of Women in its 25th Report has recommended establishment of a National Commission or similar bodies "with a mandate to review, evaluate and recommend measures and priorities to ensure equality between men and women and the full integration of women in all sectors of national life". We accordingly recommend the constitutions of statutory autonomous Commissions at the Centre and the State with the following functions:

(a) Collection of information on different matters, e.g. education, employment, health, welfare, political participation, impact of social legislation, etc., with the right to call for information on different matters from the concerned agencies of the Government and to suggest improved methods for collection of data in different fields.

(b) Evaluation of existing policies, programmes and laws that have a bearing on status of women with the following powers:

(i) To ensure non-implementation of these measures;

(ii) To point out lacunae or deficiencies in such measures and suggest amendments.

The Commission's criticisms and suggestion made after due consultation with relevant Ministries or Departments of Government should be placed before Parliament or the State Legislatures. They would be answered by the Government within a states period with explanation or assurances.

(c) Recommendations of new laws, policies or programmes aiming to implement the Directive Principles of State Policy and the objectives of the U.N. Resolutions and Conventions regarding the status of women. These should be made to Parliament or the state Legislatures and Government will be statutorily responsible to consider such recommendations for action or to explain why they cannot be accepted.

(d) Redressal of grievances in cases of actual violation of existing laws.

The Commission may be empowered to take effective steps to redress the grievances of affected parties.

Composition of the Commissions

The composition of these Commissions should be broadbased, one category being selected for their representative status from different bodies like leading women's organisations, trade unions, legislatures, employers, etc., and the other group consisting of experts from the field of law, health education, social research planning and administration. The Chairmen and the majority of the members of all the Commissions should be women. The Chairmen should be non-officials, but on a full time basis.

52. We further recommend the establishment of special Tribunals** for all violations of human rights, discrimination against women, violation or evasion of existing laws and policies for the protection of women and their rights in society.

BLUE PRINT OF ACTIONS POINTS

1. Legislative Measures

The existing legislations should be reviewed so that equality and social justice can be ensured to women of all communities and creeds. Where this involves amendments to existing personal Laws of minority group, initial efforts should be concentrated on arousing a desire for change from among the members of such minority groups. A vigorous campaign should be made to educated women about their rights, and to generate among all communities, a desire for a common civil code, to be achieved by the end of the U.N. Decade for Women in 1985.

Legal aid should be organised for women in need with the active assistance of the Bar Councils.

The setting up of family courts should be considered for speedy and effective adjudication in all cases concerning the family. Women, particularly in rural areas, should be protected against harassment.

The practice of dowry should be eradicated. The legislation should be strictly enforced. This is a social evil which requires sustained action not only on the part of Governmental agencies, but also on the part of voluntary organisations and public leaders.

The provision of the existing Child Marriage Restraint Act should be reviewed. Special attention should be given to streamlining the enforcement machinery and involving local authorities and voluntary organisations in the implementation of the Act. Active public support should be mobilised by Governmental agencies, voluntary organisations and public leaders against child marriage, particularly in rural areas. Simultaneously, systematic programmes of education and training should be developed for girls till they marry.

2. Administrative Measures

Education

Education is the greatest known catalytic agent for social change. All out efforts should therefore be made to achieve the goal of universal primary education as early as possible. The ideas of equality between the sexes and participation by women in development should be woven into the fabric of the educational system.

The employment of women teachers should be actively promoted. The existing employment procedures, including those for part-time employment, should be reviewed and, where necessary, relaxations in age, etc., made so that more women teachers, can be employed, and husbands and wives are posted in the same schools or at the same station.

The content of education should be strengthened in terms of both life and work relevance. Attention should be given to vocationalisation and diversification of courses which should not only be limited to traditional women's vocations but also give emphasis on the preparation of women for participation in modern sectors of industrial production. Polytechnics (including mini-polytechnics) should be started for girls in the smaller urban centres to provide training facilities in trades crafts which will prompt self employment.

At the stage of higher education special incentives like freeships, scholarships, hostel facilities, and book loans should be made available to girls from rural, backward and hilly areas, from backward classes and from poor families. A greater diversification in the courses offered should be made to enhance work opportunities in non-traditional vocations in modern sectors of industrial production.

Adoption of multiple entry in education, non-formal part-time education facilities condensed courses for education correspondence courses and courses for continuing education should be made available in a larger measure to women in semi-urban and rural areas, and to working women in urban and semi-urban areas. Adult education and functional literacy programmes should be vigorously pursued through both official and voluntary agencies.

3. Employment

Equal Remuneration Act, 1976, has been passed, providing for the payment of equal remuneration to men and women workers and the prevention of discrimination on grounds of sex. Special steps should therefore be taken to review recruitment, promotion another personnel practices in all public and private sector undertakings to ensure that there is no discrimination against women candidates. Women apprentices should be taken without discrimination in industries. Representatives of women's voluntary organisations should be associated in the machinery set up to ensure adequate participation of women in employment.

Village industries which provide scope for the employment of women should be further promoted. Special training services should be organised and credit, marketing facilities, etc. extended, specially in regard to crafts which can have a ready export market, through modernisation of design, etc. Integrated pilot projects to cover training, production and marketing should be started.

The existing recruitment procedures and employment conditions should be reviewed to encourage the re-entry of women into the work force. For this purpose, the provisions relating to maximum age of entry into service should be reviewed. Part-time employment of women should be promoted wherever feasible. Refresher courses and training programmes should be organised for adult women to make them fit for re-employment.

Organisations entrusted by the Government with the task of promoting self-employment opportunities should develop special women's entrepreneurial training motivation programmes and provide special assistance to women entrepreneurs and to women's co-operative in terms of credit, licensing, etc.

The existing legislation in regard to maternity benefits should be reviewed. It should simultaneously be ensured that there is no consequent adverse effect on the employment of women.

4. Health Care, Nutrition and Family Planning

Maternal and child health care facilities should be expanded, particularly in semi-urban and rural areas, and coverage provided to high risk pregnant women. Ante-natal and post-natal clinics should be started in every Primary Health Centre and district hospital.

Nutrition supplementation should be provided to high risk pregnant mothers. Simultaneously, nutrition and health education should be given to girls and to mothers through all available media and institutions (school, hospitals, PHCs, etc.)

Family welfare planning services should be expanded and measures intensified to educate and prepare couples to avail them, specifically in rural, backward and tribal areas. The facilities under the Medical Termination of Pregnancy Act, 1971 should be made available in semi-urban and rural areas and information regarding the provisions disseminated among women, immunisation facilities should be gradually extended to all children.

Facilities of Working Women

The establishment of day-care centres, creches, and balwadis should be promoted on a large scale in rural, semi-urban and urban areas to help working mothers and active women social workers discharge their duties, and enable the older children to attend school.

Hostel facilities for working women of the lower income groups should be expanded.

Care for the Socially Disadvantaged

Women without any means of support, and the physically handicapped should be provided services for education, training and rehabilitation so that they can become self-reliant. Old age homes should be opened for the aged and the infirm. Special programmes should be developed for unmarried mothers and their children.

The provision of the Suppression of Immoral Traffic Act (1956) should be reviewed to facilitate their more efficient implementation. Comprehensive rehabilitation programmes for victims of immoral traffic and their children should de developed. Special steps should be taken to prevent vulnerable young girls and women from becoming victims of this social evil.

Bibliography

Altbach, Edith Hoshino (1974), *Women in America,* D.C. Heath and Co.

Altekar, A.S. (1978), *The Position of Women in Hindu Civilisation,* Motilal Banarasidass, Delhi.

Baboo Ishuree Dass (1960), *Domestic Manners and Customs of the Hindoos of North India,* Medical Hall Press, Banaras.

Baig, Tara Ali, *India's women power,* S. Chand and Co. (P) Ltd., New Delhi, 1976.

Brinkerhoff, Robert O. (1986), Brinkerhoff, Robert O.: *Expanding Needs Analysis, Training and Development Journal. American Society for Training and Development* (ASID) Inc., Alexendria, Va., February, 1964-65.

Chapman, Jane Roberts (1976), *Economic independence for women: The foundation for equal rights,* Vol. I, Sage Publication.

Dandiya, C.K. (ed.) (1975), *Women in Rajasthan;* University of Rajasthan.

Davis, Delia (1976), *Woman-work,* Oxford University Press,

Desai, M.G. and Gaikwad, V.R. (1971), *ANP : An Evaluation Study,* Centre for Management in Agri., IIM, Ahmedabad, pp. 135 and 189.

Dev Ram, Lal Bindiya (1982), *Monitoring and Evaluation*

of Community Participation in an ICDS Project, Unpublished Report, NIPCCD, New Delhi.

Devaki Jain (ed.) (1975),*Indian Women,* Publications Division, Ministry of Information and Broadcasting Government of India, New Delhi.

Gandhi, T.B. (1984),*Community Participation in the Urban ICDS Project Vizag, Andhra Pradesh,* Deptt. of Paediatrics, Andhra Med. College, Visakhapatnam, A.P.

Ganguli, B.N. (1979), *Emma Goldman, Portrait of a Rebel Women,* Allied Publishers Pvt. Ltd., New Delhi.

Govt. of India (1956), *Summary Record of Fifth Development Commissioners' Conference held at Nainital,* (5-7th May 1956), p. 58.

Govt. of India (1978),*Report of the Committee on Panchayati Raj Institutions* (Chairman : Asoka Mehta), Deptt. of Rural Development, Min. of Agri. and Irri., August, pp. 141-142.

Govt. of India (1982), *Integrated Child Development Services Scheme (Revised),* Ministry of Social Welfare, New Delhi, p. 2-3.

Govt. of Maharashtra (1971), *Report of the Evaluation Committee on ANP,* Deptt. of Rural Development, pp. 18-20.

Hate, C.A. (1969), *Changing status of women in post-independence India,* Allied Publishers.

Jain, S.P. (1979), *Role of Women in Rural Development - A Study of Mahila Mandals,* NIRD, Hyderabad, p. 4.

Jain, S.P. (1982) , *Bhartiya Grameen Mahila Sangh - A Case Study,* NIRD, Hyderabad.

K.M. Kapadia (1972), *Marriage and Family in India,* Oxford University Press, Calcutta,.

Kapur, Promilla (1970), *Marriage and the working women in India,* Vikas Publishing House.

Kapur, Promilla (1974), *The changing status of the working women in India,* Vikas Publishing House.

Kumar, Salil (1987), Psychological Correlates of Management Development Training Programmes. Doctoral Thesis (Unpublished,) IIT Delhi, New Delhi.

Lakshi Misra (1966), 'Education of Women in India: 1921-1966'.

Mager, R.F. and Pipe, P. (1989), *Analyzing performance problems.* Palo Alto. California; Fearon Publishers.

Maria Mies (1980). *Indian Women and Patriarchy,* Concept Publishing Company, New Delhi.

Mathur, R.N. (1989)., Quality of Working Life of Women Construction Workers, Commonwealth Publishers, New Delhi.

Murthy, L.S.N. and Mathur, S. (1988) : *Project Management - A Study of ICDS Projects,* NIPCCD, New Delhi.

Muthayya, B.C. and et. al. (1978) : *Evaluation of ANP,* Interim Report presented at National Seminar on ANP Held at NIRD, Hyderabad.

Myrdal, Alva and Kelin, Viola (1956), *Women's two roles: Home and Work,* Routledge and Kegan Paul.

Nanda, B.R. (ed.) (1976), *Indian women from purdah to modernity,* Vikas Publishing House.

P. Thomas (1964), *Indian Woman Through the Ages,* Asia Publishing House, Bombay.

Paranjpe, Rajni K. and Bhagwat, Rewati (1984), *A Study of Perception and Participation of the Community in ICDS in Maharashtra,* Unpublished, Mimeograph, College of Social Work, Bombay.

Ranade, S.N. and Ramachandran P. (1970), *Women and employment,* Bombay, Tata Institute of Social Sciences.

Reddy, Kumari (1972), *Problems of married working women with particular reference to Tirupati,* Thesis submitted for M.Sc. Home Science, S.V. University, Tirupati.

Rummler, G.A. (1976) The performance audit. Training and Development Handbook (2nd ed.), McGraw Hill, N.Y..

Sethi, Raj Mohini (1976), *Modernisation of Working Women in developing societies,* National Publishing House.

Shakuntala Jayal (1966), *The Status of Women in the Epics,* Motilal Banarasidass, Patna.

Shridharan N., (1989), Whither Democratic Planning: Some Issues,' in Ashok Kumar and R.P. Mamgain (ed.), *Manpower Planning in India,* Criterion Publications, New Delhi.

Smuts, Robert, W. (1959), *Woman and work in America,* Columbia University Books Inc.

Tara Ali Baig (1976), *India's Woman Power,* S. Chand & Co. Pvt. Ltd., New Delhi.

Vasu, E. (1990), 'Mahilasamajam Movement in Kerala,' *Social Welfare,* Vol. XXVII, No. 7, Oct. pp. 20-33.

Index

●●●